Praise for *You, Me and Autism*

"As someone whose passions are learning, reading, and working with autistic people and their families, I tremendously enjoyed reading You, Me, and Autism. The book creates and paints different and unique worlds through elegant and evocative stories, taking the reader through a fulfilling journey of discovery. As such, it can be viewed as a significant literary work. Importantly, to everyone interested in learning about autism from the perspectives of the families, this book offers invaluable insights and should therefore be essential reading for the general public, students, clinicians, researchers, and policymakers. Although I have worked in the field of autism for a significant period of time, I have benefited greatly from the diverse perspectives presented in this excellent book. We need more books like this."

— **Mirko Uljarevic, MD, PhD,** Associate Professor of Psychiatry and Behavioral Sciences, Stanford University

"Using research evidence and diverse lived experiences this is a beautiful exploration of autistic identity as well as practical strategies. It takes a strengths-based approach to understanding autism from core characteristics to daily living, schooling, employment, relationships, disclosure, and well-being."

— **Dane Dougan,** Chief Executive Officer, Autism New Zealand

You, Me, and Autism

How to Support, Befriend, and Work with Autistic People

Phoebe Jordan

You, Me, and Autism: How to Support, Befriend, and Work with Autistic People
Copyright © 2025 by Phoebe Jordan

All rights reserved. No part of this book may be used or reproduced in any manner whatsoever without written permission except in the case of brief quotations embodied in articles and reviews, in accordance with US Fair Use law. For information, contact the publisher.

Published by Upriver Press
Colorado Springs, Colorado
upriverpress.com

Cover Design: James Clarke (jclarke.net)

ISBN Print Version: 9798990623620
ISBN Ebook: 9798990623637

Library of Congress Control Number: 2025933949

Printed in the United States of America.

Upriver Press publishes books by leading scholars and industry experts who bring well-researched, evidence-based ideas to public discourse. The views of our authors do not necessarily represent the opinions of Upriver Press staff, distributors, or printers.

You, Me, and Autism

How to Support, Befriend, and Work with Autistic People

Phoebe Jordan

Contents

Introduction	7
1. Language	11
2. Identity	19
3. Sensory Experiences	35
4. Meltdowns and Shutdowns	69
5. Mental Health	75
6. Relationships	83
7. Education and Employment	109
8. Disclosure	123
9. Symphony of Life	137
Epilogue	157
Acknowledgements	161
About the Author	163
Appendix	165
Bibliography	167
Index	187

Introduction

Here is a common saying: "If you've met one autistic person, then you've met one autistic person." This book is a testament to that diversity. According to research, approximately one child out of every thirty-six in America is diagnosed as autistic. Each is unique. This statistic underscores the importance of understanding and embracing neurodiversity, which is at the heart of this book's purpose. By combining academic research with my personal experiences and the diverse narratives of other autistic individuals, I provide practical strategies and scholarly insights. Whether you are autistic, a loved one, or a professional, this book offers valuable perspectives and tools for fostering understanding and support.

In addition to sharing my personal experiences as an autistic person, I have incorporated narratives from others who have graciously allowed me to present their stories. I refer to them with pseudonyms. They represent different genders, ages of diagnosis, communication methods, and life experiences, but there are many other types of autistic people. The scholarly and personal perspectives shared in the book do not represent the entirety of the autistic community. However, I believe they will contribute to the broader understanding of autism and its multifaceted nature. I hope this book serves as a starting point for illuminating the richness and diversity within the autism spectrum. Without painting autism as a tragedy or being pollyannaish, I aim to present a balanced perspective about the strengths and challenges that autistic people experience.

This book will also provide strategies to support autistic

individuals and those who have autistic people in their lives. *You, Me, and Autism* will help bridge the understanding gap between autistic and allistic individuals. The strategies have proven to be helpful in most cases, but not every strategy will be effective for everyone all the time. Autism exists on a spectrum, so no solution can be applied universally. As people grow and evolve, and as their situations change, they will need different strategies at different times in life. For this reason, readers will benefit from periodically revisiting the book with a focus on the sections that are most relevant at each stage of life. Because these changes affect the autistic person's friends, professional colleagues, and loved ones, I also encourage you to use the book as source for deeper conversations. You can think of the book as a *personal* autism toolkit.

These strategies are helpful tools, but they should not be forced on anyone, nor should they be used with the intent of trying to "fix" someone. My purpose is to raise awareness and advance understanding of the diverse experiences of autistic individuals, not run a repair shop. Every person, whether autistic or allistic, is a valuable, meaningful, and loved individual. No one is broken, and no one needs to be fixed or cured. We are all beautifully unique in our own way.

Before diving into the content of this book, I first need to address the crucial issue of language. Within the autism community, there is some debate about whether to use identity-first language (e.g., an autistic person) or person-first language (e.g., a person with autism). I will explore this topic further in the following chapter, but for the sake of immediate clarity, I have chosen to use identity-first language, which is the preference of most people in the autistic community, including myself. Throughout this book, I will write

Introduction

about "autistic people" or "autistic individuals."

When referring to people who are not autistic, I will usually use the word *allistic*. I have opted not to use *neurotypical*. If I solely referred to people as either neurotypical or autistic, I would inadvertently exclude many other neurodiverse people with a wide range of brain types, including ADHD, OCD, and others.

Next, allow me to introduce you to four autistic individuals who have graciously shared their stories for this book.

Meet Sam, an eighteen-year-old autistic male who received his diagnosis when he was nine. He lives at home with his parents, twin brother, and two cats. Sam communicates through speaking and sign language. He enjoys building giant Lego sculptures, including an impressive Lego version of the *Titanic*.

Emma is a twenty-four-year-old autistic female who received her diagnosis at age twenty-three. Emma lives in her flat with her partner and cat. She loves TV shows, all things beautiful, singing, and baking.

Third, we have Helen, a nineteen-year-old autistic woman who was diagnosed when she was four. Helen responded to my interview questions using a mixture of sign language, writing, and speaking. She enjoys reading and spending time outside in nature.

Finally, we have Nate, a devoted father of two who lives with his children and wife. Nate cherishes quality time with his family and friends, finding joy in the everyday moments they spend together.

I will also share my own story. As an autistic person, I have navigated through the challenges and joys of discovering and embracing my identity. My passion for raising awareness and providing practical, everyday strategies for both autistic and allistic individuals drives my writing and scholarly work. I believe in the power of understanding and acceptance to foster a more inclusive and supportive society for everyone.

CHAPTER 1

Language

There are two primary ways to refer to an autistic individual: person-first language and identity-first language. Person-first language emphasizes the individual before the condition (e.g., a person with autism), whereas identity-first language emphasizes the condition as an integral part of the individual (e.g., an autistic person). The distinction between these two approaches is not merely semantic; it reflects deeper attitudes and beliefs about autism. It is crucial to respect each autistic person's preference. Listening to and honoring our choices acknowledges our identities and fosters a more inclusive and respectful environment. Being mindful of this choice shows consideration for our autonomy and contributes to a supportive community.

Person-first language places individuals before their condition in a sentence, such as saying, "I am a person with autism." This approach aims to emphasize individuality rather than defining people by their condition. Some individuals prefer person-first language because it highlights that autism alone does not define us. It shows others that we are unique individuals with our own strengths, challenges, and interests. The person-first perspective originated from the medical field, which historically attached negative connotations to autism and other disabilities and differences. In the past, doctors often referred to autism with words like *symptoms, deficits, atypical, abnormal,* or *problem.* These terms have propagated throughout society. As a result, people sought to separate the individual from these negative associations by using person-first language. Research indicates that professionals and parents are more likely to use person-first language because they want to promote a more positive and humanizing view of autism.

On the other hand, identity-first language embraces autism as an inherent part of a person's identity. Autism is not seen as something separate from the person. Many autistic individuals advocate against person-first language, which to them feels dehumanizing because it implies that autism is a detachable or secondary trait. We argue that you cannot separate a person from their autism because autism is an intrinsic part of who we are. Autism fundamentally shapes our experiences, perceptions, and interactions with the world. So, an identity-first perspective emphasizes that autism is not an appendage; rather, it is a core aspect of identity, deserving recognition and respect. Identity-first language also encourages acceptance and pride within the autistic community. It helps autistic individuals to assert their right to be seen and accepted for who they are, without implying that they need to be fixed or that their autism is something to be downplayed.

Research shows that most autistic individuals prefer identity-first language. For me and many others, being autistic is an integral part of our identity. Therefore, identity-first language conveys our self-acceptance, fostering a sense of pride in our neurodiversity. The emphasis on self-acceptance aligns with the broader goals of the neurodiversity movement, which advocates for accepting and celebrating all neurological variations as natural and valuable aspects of human diversity. By choosing identity-first language, we challenge the societal norms that seek to marginalize or pathologize autistic individuals, and we promote a more inclusive and affirming

Language

view of autism.

When discussing this topic with my father, he sought to understand the identity-first perspective better by thinking through the alternative. He said, "I am a short person, not a person with short. But if I have leprosy, then I am a person with leprosy, not a leprosy person." His analogy leads to my next point, which relates to the idea of *curing* autism. Using person-first language can imply that autism is something that needs to be cured. By contrast, we typically say that people have cancer or have a broken leg because these are conditions we aim to cure or fix. Autism, however, is not something that needs to be fixed; it is a natural part of human diversity that enriches the world. It is a unique flavor in the grand recipe of humanity. Thus, by emphasizing autism as an integral aspect of a person's identity we can avoid viewing it as a condition that needs a cure; instead, we can recognize it as a unique and valuable way of experiencing the world. We can see autism as an operating system that comes with remarkable features.

There is another reason to use identity-first language. The positive attributes of people are usually placed before the person, such as "a beautiful person" or "a smart person," rather than "a person with beauty" or "a person with smart." Thus, when we place the word *autism* after the word *person,* we perpetuate the notion that autism is a negative attribute. However, autism is not a negative attribute or a disability; it is a unique configuration of our brains. Autism encompasses a wide range of experiences, strengths, and perspectives that enrich our communities and contribute to the diversity of human thought and creativity. This perspective is central to the neurodiversity movement, which advocates for recognizing and celebrating the diverse ways in which human brains can function. By valuing neurodiversity, we challenge the conventional notions of normalcy and expand our understanding of human potential.

As you can see, the language we use significantly influences and reflects how we perceive autism and cognitive diversity. Some words can spread the stigmatization of autistic people, causing them to be marginalized. By contrast, a society that affirms neurodiversity will accept our differences as *valuable characteristics* or *traits*. Neurological differences are natural variations in the human genome, not deficiencies to be corrected. By using accurate language that reflects that truth, we can shift societal perceptions and promote a more inclusive and accepting environment. Then society can benefit from the contributions of neurodivergent individuals.

Problems with using the wrong language can appear early in the autism diagnosis process. Diagnostic words are often deficit-based, making the process feel draining and traumatic. When I was screened for autism, the professionals told me that I was "at risk of autism" and that I "had symptoms aligned with autism." The term *risk* implied danger or harm, and *symptoms* suggested that I needed to cure an illness.

A more positive framing would have sounded like this: "You have a high likelihood of being autistic" or "You are showing signs of being autistic." This type of positive framing reduces stigma. It promotes an accurate understanding of autism as a natural variation in human neurology rather than as a threat or a problem to be solved. Proper wording during the diagnostic process empowers self-acceptance and identity. What if diagnostic professionals could help autistic people understand that they have just joined an exclusive club of unique thinkers rather than making them feel like a medical mystery in need of a cure? Positive, accurate language can also be affirming for the families of autistic people. And, in alignment with the neurodiversity movement, a positive approach to diagnosis will help shift societal perceptions, promoting a broader cultural acceptance of neurodiversity.

People sometimes describe autistic individuals as "suffering from autism." This is not accurate. I do not suffer from autism; I am autistic. I *did* suffer from a broken leg when I was eleven. Being autistic simply means I have different strengths and challenges compared to an allistic person, but being autistic is not inherently negative or positive. Autism is a fundamental aspect of who I am, shaping my experiences and perspectives. I can approach problems creatively, perceive the world in novel ways, and develop deep, specialized knowledge in my areas of interest. Labeling autism as something one *suffers* from reinforces a negative stereotype and overlooks the unique strengths and positive attributes that come with being autistic.

Within discussions about autism, we also hear modifier words like *mild, high functioning, low functioning,* or *more autistic.* These terms are used to describe how a person functions in everyday life, but these labels can be misleading. They do not accurately capture the complexity of an individual's experiences and needs. People who have been labeled as high functioning, for example, are often perceived as being better able to blend into society. However, it could be that the autistic person is working hard to "camouflage" (cover or hide) traits that are rarely accepted in social settings. (See more about camouflaging in chapter 2.) Thus, allistic people often do not see the full reality of autistic people.

These labels further stigmatize autistic individuals and

invalidate their needs. Words that misrepresent the reality of autistic people can delay a diagnosis and necessary support. If autistic individuals are labeled as high functioning, they may quietly struggle without receiving the help they require. This can be harmful in educational, professional, and social contexts, where support is crucial for success and well-being. Conversely, those labeled as low functioning might be unjustly deemed incapable, which means they will have fewer opportunities for growth, independence, and professional development.

These labels can also negatively impact an autistic person's self-esteem and sense of identity. Being labeled as high functioning might pressure autistic people to constantly strive for unrealistic expectations, causing stress and burnout. Those labeled as low functioning might internalize negative perceptions about their capabilities and self-worth. By understanding and avoiding these labels, we can better support autistic individuals in a way that respects their unique needs and potential.

Many autistic people, me included, have noticed a common reaction when we share our autism diagnosis with other people. They often respond with something like, "Oh, we are all on the spectrum." Or they might say, "Everyone is a bit autistic." These comments are inaccurate. A person cannot be "a bit autistic." Either a person is autistic or not. I understand that allistic people might say these things to offer comfort and express solidarity, but these types of statements invalidate the reality of being autistic. We need to recognize that autistic individuals view and experience the world differently. Overlooking these differences—by saying that all people are "a bit autistic"— can prevent autistic people from receiving the support they need. Without that support, they might struggle more

Language

with sensory overload, social confusion, cognitive challenges, mental health issues, and burnout.

I will discuss these issues later in the book, but the improper use of language can make it harder for autistic people to manage these aspects of life. For example, autistic burnout, which is beyond typical exhaustion, is a prolonged period of feeling overwhelmed and fatigued. During a period of burnout, autistic people may lose interest in their favorite activities, suffer from decreased executive functioning, and struggle to manage sensory input. Burnout does not reflect a lack of motivation; rather, it is the result of being completely exhausted by relentless demands. When they lose motivation, they experience a profound disconnection from themselves. The whole experience can be terribly distressing.

Using proper language can reduce the chances of an autistic burnout. We must move away from using terms like high functioning and low functioning. Instead, we should seek a deeper understanding of each person's experiences and needs. Some may need more assistance with social interactions, while others might require more help with managing sensory processes. Autistic individuals should not have to continuously struggle against societal misconceptions about their needs or face barriers to receiving help. They need a personalized approach that respects their unique challenges and strengths.

Furthermore, the misuse of language can create a divide within the autistic community. For example, when some autistic individuals are labeled as high functioning and others as low functioning, it can lead to feelings of exclusion and stigmatization. Those deemed to be low functioning may feel shunned or be told they need to be fixed. Those deemed to be high functioning might be more accepted in social circles, but their less-visible needs could be overlooked. So, we should avoid using labels. They are not medical terms; they are pointless societal constructs that can harm people by oversimplifying their unique experiences, contributions, and needs. By focusing on individual experiences rather than generalized terms, we can better appreciate the diversity within the autistic community and provide tailored and effective support.

It is essential to have a discussion with autistic individuals about the words they prefer and then respect those preferences. I recommend that allistic people ask autistic coworkers, friends, and family members about their preferences. Specifically, try to understand whether the autistic person prefers person-first language (a person with autism) or identity-first language (an autistic person) and respect the choice. Language preferences and perspectives can evolve, so be willing to learn. Consider the impact of your words and avoid using terms or phrases that can stigmatize or marginalize autistic individuals.

CHAPTER 2

Identity

When asked to describe themselves, autistic people frequently say they are creative, loyal, funny, honest, strong, authentic, different, lonely, problem solvers, positive, peaceful, organized, intelligent, survivors, quiet, tired, caring, outgoing (when comfortable around people), fun and adventurous, kind, independent, hardworking, introverted, passionate for learning, and nature loving.

Likewise, allistic people frequently say that their autistic friends and family members are pure, joyful, creative, different, amazing, awesome, friendly, organized, empathetic, intelligent, loving and good, happy being themselves, compassionate, encouraging, caring, courageous, warm, affectionate, beautiful, positive, thoughtful, and full of light.

What words would you use to describe *yourself?*

The language we use to describe ourselves both influences and reflects our sense of identity. We form our identities as we grow. Identity encompasses our experiences, emotions, memories, interests, relationships, values, and ways of existing. Because life is always changing, our identities develop over time. Whether we encourage or hinder that development depends on how we express our emotions, memories, interests, and values. We also need support from others to help us discover ourselves and grow.

I grew up not knowing how I could ever fit into the world. I felt like a shadow of a person, or like a leaf easily swept away by the wind. But when I received my autism diagnosis, I saw my life through a new lens. It felt liberating to know that I was not broken or alone. I could begin to see myself as a whole person, full of likes, dislikes, experiences, and memories—just like every other autistic person and every other human. Understanding my diagnosis helped me embrace my identity and begin to find my place in the world.

After the diagnosis, I did not know how to begin exploring my identity. I was unsure about what to experiment with or how to go about it. My journey began by recognizing what made me feel good and what made me feel bad. I realized that putting a "mask" on every day was painful and left me feeling lost in the world. So, I started experimenting with different ways of dressing and styling myself to discover what I truly wanted and how I could express myself authentically in ways that brought me joy.

Autistic and allistic people need to cultivate their identities with care. It is a long and complex process. We all must embrace our beliefs and then choose to uphold them. We should not abandon our beliefs just to fit in. The same is true for autistic individuals. Embracing one's true self, including all the unique autistic traits and characteristics, is essential for building a positive and resilient identity.

For many autistic people, the process of exploring their identities can be obstructed by societal pressures that attempt to squeeze them into a neurotypical mold. Autistic people often encounter barriers against their ability to live authentically. These barriers can include difficulties with processing emotions or struggling to correctly interpret what others mean during conversations. As a result, many autistic individuals resort to what is called *camouflaging*. In this case, a person might hide or suppress the true self to fit in with societal expectations. Camouflaging can be

Identity

categorized in two forms.

The first is *masking*. This involves suppressing common autistic traits, such as *stimming*, which refers to self-stimulatory behaviors like repetitive hand flapping, rocking, or other movements that help autistic individuals manage sensory input or emotions. Autistic people often mask these behaviors to appear more neurotypical, often at the expense of their own comfort and well-being.

The second form of camouflaging is *compensating*, which occurs when an autistic person consciously adopts (or imitates) neurotypical social behaviors to be accepted in social settings. These behaviors might include maintaining eye contact, mimicking facial expressions, or using scripted conversations. These behaviors do not seem natural to most autistic people, but they might be useful for avoiding social marginalization.

Making eye contact is often the first mimicking behavior that comes to an autistic individual's mind. During conversations, I am acutely aware of whether I am making eye contact. If I catch myself avoiding eye contact, I physically "drag" my eyes back into connection. The work of constant self-monitoring is mentally exhausting.

For me, compensating also involves scripting my conversations before I meet with people. I rehearse my wording. I practice my body language, my voice tones, and my facial expressions, in part by drawing inspiration from TV shows. (Binge-watching Netflix can be educational!) I spend time observing the behaviors and speech patterns of people around me. I prepare for phone calls by scripting my responses in notebooks. This meticulous preparation is an attempt to align my behaviors with societal expectations, ensuring that I come across as "normal."

Helen told me that she uses similar compensating techniques in social situations. She prepares and rehearses specific phrases and responses for common interactions. She has set responses and facial expressions ready for small-talk questions like, "How are you?" and "What do you do for work?" She practices these responses before attending social events. This preparation provides her with a safety net, reducing her anxiety, but it can also feel restrictive and meaningless, preventing genuine interaction and connection. Helen also expends great effort to maintain eye contact during conversations, despite feeling uncomfortable. She tries to focus on the other person's nose or forehead as a substitute, but this technique can be draining and distracting, making it difficult to concentrate on the conversation itself. The pressure to maintain eye contact while keeping up with the dialogue adds an extra layer of stress, further reinforcing the challenges that come with camouflaging.

Autistic individuals have many ways of compensating and adapting to social norms. We all have our own survival skills toolkit. Regardless of the method, all forms of compensating require autistic people *to suppress their true identities*. That is the deepest struggle for us. Constantly pushed to imitate others, we rely on borrowed behaviors, which can feel hollow, fake, and unfulfilling. The energy we spend on maintaining a façade could be better invested in expressing our true selves.

Autistic individuals often use masking and compensating strategies to avoid negative judgments and misunderstandings. However, some autistic people rely on these methods because they have experienced years of severe torment and trauma. Many have unfortunately endured extensive bullying and harassment, especially during their formative years. These traumatic experiences impose a

Identity

long-term underlying fear of abuse, which in turn compels them to protect themselves by mimicking societal norms.

Nate told me that he feels compelled to camouflage his true self even when he is around his parents, siblings, and some extended family members. He wants to avoid judgmental feedback, so he withdraws and stops talking, or he relies on a script to communicate what he thinks will be socially appropriate. However, he feels he is not being true to himself.

Sam shared with me his camouflaging experience during college. Each time someone noticed something different about him, that person would make him feel uncomfortable. To avoid this discomfort, he worked hard to act in a way that helped him fit in and avoid rejection. Every day, Sam hid his true feelings, faked a smile, and endured the soul-crushing experience of pretending to be someone other than himself—all to avoid judgment, ostracization, and abuse. The emotional toll on Sam was intense.

Helen resorts to camouflaging to avoid negative reactions or misunderstandings. She feels as though this tactic is almost automatic now, because she has forced herself to do it for so many years. She uses techniques like mimicking others' social behaviors, practicing conversations ahead of time, and using scripts for common social interactions. The constant need to use camouflaging methods becomes a deeply ingrained habit, making it difficult for her to be free and authentic.

Identity and Special Interests

In the previous chapter, I wrote about the meaning that special interests have in the lives of autistic people. These interests can provide a sense of purpose, joy, and fulfilment. In addition, they help provide a foundation for personal development and identity.

Autistic people usually focus intently on just a few special interests. This might seem odd to allistic people, who often think that a deep commitment to a singular passion is limiting or obsessive. Therefore, allistic people often urge autistic friends and family members to explore a broader range of activities. This pressure can feel like an invalidation of our passions, suggesting that our natural inclinations are somehow insufficient or inappropriate. That cuts deep because, for autistic individuals, our special interests are central to our identities and well-being. These activities offer a deep sense of satisfaction that can be difficult to find elsewhere.

The invalidation of special interests can hinder an autistic person's growth, self-understanding, knowledge, self-confidence, and resilience. Special interests often act as a source of comfort and stability, providing a reliable refuge, an opportunity to be immersed in a deeply meaningful activity. Unfortunately, when pressured to conform to other opinions, autistic individuals may feel compelled to hide their true interests, leading to a loss of connection with a vital part of their identities. This suppression can result in feelings of emptiness or disorientation because the individual is forced to live without the grounding influence of their passions.

Additionally, special interests can be a powerful tool for connecting with others who share similar passions. In a supportive environment, these interests can foster meaningful relationships and community bonds. As autistic people share their passions, they find open doors to deep and lasting connections. Therefore, it is important for allistic people to celebrate the special interests of autistic people as a means of helping them find a more prosperous and authentic life.

Identity and Clothing

I discovered the joy of expressing my identity through clothing. I sometimes enjoy wearing tight clothing because the pressure helps me stay emotionally regulated. At other times, I prefer loose clothing because I simply cannot stand anything touching me. Instead of focusing on what people tell me I should wear or copying others to fit in, I now focus on what feels like an expression of my identity. I prioritize comfort and authentic self-expression.

Like many autistic people, I previously used clothing, makeup, and hairstyle as ways to camouflage. I spent hours observing and copying what others wore, applying makeup, and styling my hair in ways I thought would help me fit in. Each day, putting on my outfit felt like putting on a mask. That might sound like I was trying to be a secret agent, but the effort was not as cool as that. There were no fancy gadgets or thrilling car chases, just a lot of eyeliner and wardrobe changes. I remember looking in the mirror and not recognizing the person staring back at me. It felt like I was a stranger to myself, fragmented and pulled in so many different directions that nothing was left of my true self. My disguises might have helped me navigate social situations, but they also made me feel like I was living someone else's life—and not a particularly exciting one. No thrilling heists or daring escapes, just the daily grind of trying to fit in. In the end, I realized that the best mission I could undertake was to discover and embrace my true self, even if it meant stepping out of the safety net of my disguise.

I gradually realized that by embracing my own clothing style—tight or loose, makeup or no makeup—I could step toward reclaiming and expressing my identity. This shift helped me feel more like myself and reduced the mental and emotional toll of maintaining a façade. Embracing my true self through clothing has been a crucial element of my journey toward self-acceptance and mental well-being. The journey involves trial and error, discovering what feels right and what does not. We all need to be patient with ourselves as we go through life.

Identity and Movement

Allistic people rarely think about their bodily movements in daily social settings, but autistic people are always worried about how to disguise their authentic movements to fit in. For me, stimming and the use of fidget toys often attract more attention than my clothing choices. I used to minimize my stimming by relying on subtle actions like finger tapping and hand squeezing, which were easier to hide and attracted fewer comments. I did not want to move in ways that were different than the movements of those around me. I remember being aware of this tension by no later than age five. However, suppressing these natural movements made me feel uncomfortable in my own skin. I felt disconnected from my

Identity

body, resulting in heightened anxiety, skin picking, and nail biting.

As I grew older, I came to realize the importance of allowing myself to stim freely and to use fidget toys without shame. This freedom has allowed me to feel at ease with myself, which has significantly reduced my anxiety. Finding and using fidget toys that suit my needs—a stress ball, a tangle toy, or a simple rubber band—has felt empowering. Each tool has provided a unique way to channel my energy and maintain focus. Incorporating these items into my daily routine, without worrying about societal judgments, has allowed me to reclaim a part of myself that I had previously suppressed. Now that I have given myself the freedom to move in ways that feel right for me, I have come to realize that keeping my body still had been preventing me from truly feeling my emotions.

Furthermore, integrating movement into my daily routine has enhanced my overall well-being. Activities like yoga, dancing, and stretching have become integral parts of my life, promoting physical health and emotional balance. These practices offer avenues for self-expression and personal growth, further shaping my identity.

My close-knit community now accepts and enjoys my "happy hands," dancing, bouncing, and squeezing stims. I have become quite the source of entertainment! Who needs TV when you can be around my spontaneous dance moves? This newfound freedom has helped me explore my identity and get to know my true self. I feel like I have discovered a hidden superpower; instead of flying or becoming invisible, I get to experience the joy of being unapologetically me. People close to me have become more understanding and supportive, recognizing the importance of these movements in my life.

Identity and Community

Academic research and the experiences of autistic people indicate that external support and acceptance are critical for them to develop a positive identity. Many autistic individuals have found that the most impactful support comes from within the autistic community. Facebook groups for autistic people, online and offline autistic advocates, and blogs and books written by autistic writers can significantly contribute to fostering a positive view of oneself.

Sam, Emma, Nate, Helen, and I all share the desire to meet and interact with more people like us, strengthening our connections with the autistic community, which feels comfortable and fosters a sense of belonging. In addition to in-person gatherings, we can meet online. We enjoy sharing life stories and perhaps picking up useful tips from each other. Without the pressure to conform to neurotypical societal norms, we are free to appreciate and explore our diversity, which improves mental and emotional well-being. We can express ourselves authentically, experiment with new ways of being, and receive validation from others who understand us.

Beyond these types of communities, autistic people also need support from allistic friends, family, and colleagues. This means that allistic people need to create environments in which autistic people are valued and understood for who they are, without fear of judgment or rejection. Through connections with allistic people, everyone can learn that our differences are not deficits but strengths. However, this means that allistic people need to accept behaviors that are natural for autistic people. Sometimes these behaviors can be difficult for allistic people to understand.

Identity

What happens in a social setting if allistic people do not understand the reasons for stimming? How would they interpret those behaviors? Without knowledge, allistic people might conclude that the autistic person is not paying attention or is not interested in a conversation. That would be an erroneous conclusion based on false assumptions. In fact, stimming is a way to be *more engaged* in conversations. For us, sitting still requires intense focus on our bodily sensations, and that can hinder our ability to absorb information effectively. Stimming helps autistic people to concentrate less on the body and more on what is being said. Allistic people need to recognize that physical movement helps autistic people think, converse, concentrate, and listen.

By contrast, camouflaging imposes a significant cognitive burden on autistic people, which makes it difficult for them to engage in conversations and activities. Continuous self-surveillance leads to exhaustion, anxiety, and a diminished sense of self. The effort to conform to expected behaviors leads to superficial interactions. The autistic individual withdraws mentally and emotionally from relational interactions. We might miss important information or struggle to respond appropriately during conversations because our focus is split between managing appearances and trying to engage with those around us. And under all that weight, we still deal with a perpetual fear of being judged or misunderstood. We become trapped in a cycle of self-censorship and hypervigilance, which is difficult to escape.

When autistic people become overwhelmed with stress and exhaustion, they often need to withdraw. Allistic people, failing to understand everything that an autistic person is experiencing, might interpret this behavior as rudeness or selfishness—an unwillingness to contribute to the group. When I mention that my social battery is drained, or when I express anxiety about a social situation, people frequently tell me to "get over it," or "don't be rude," or "just grow up." (Because it's that simple, right?) These comments invalidate my emotions and perspectives, leaving me to feel unaccepted and misunderstood. The lack of validation can increase the experience of profound isolation. I feel even more pressure to use camouflaging strategies to hide my true self, leading to a sense of failure and self-doubt. Each instance of masking chips away at my self-esteem, reinforcing the belief that my natural way of being is fundamentally flawed. It is like repeatedly trying to fit a square peg into a round hole. So, next time someone tells me to "just get over it," I might hand them a square peg and ask them to fit it into a round hole—because that is exactly how it feels.

Allistic people also need to understand that perpetual camouflaging can cause autistic people to experience a sense of disconnection from *themselves*. When autistic people spend years imitating others, they might lose touch with their own preferences, sources of enjoyment, desires, beliefs, and values. These personal losses increase the difficulty of making decisions or setting boundaries. Pressure to fit in and the fear of rejection can result in chronic stress, which can impact mental health and physical health (e.g., fatigue, insomnia, and other stress-related conditions). When the world constantly tells you that everything you do is wrong, it is natural to develop a negative self-image—the loss of self.

As allistic people interact with their autistic friends, family members, and coworkers, they have a role in creating nonjudgemental, inclusive, and healthy relational environments. So much is at stake *for everyone*. Increased autism awareness and

Identity

advocacy can help allistic people recognize and celebrate the unique strengths and perspectives that come with being autistic.

To help autistic people connect well in a broader community, I recommend that each autistic person create a "board of trustees." I do not mean a group of people in suits who are sitting at a big table. They should be trusted individuals who are reliable, who have the autistic person's best interests at heart, and who can offer guidance and support in various aspects of life.

For all people—autistic or otherwise—the formation of identity is entwined with community. So, we must work together to create communities in which everyone is accepted, validated, and supported.

The Strengths of Autistic Identity

When asked what it means to be autistic, Nate said that it is a way of processing and functioning in daily life in a manner that suits him. Emma told me that it means her brain is slightly different than most, so her way of processing experiences is unique. Sam said that being autistic means he is a unique person. Although he has some disabilities, they make him who he is. He would not want to live without any of them. Helen described being autistic as seeing the world in uncommon ways, and she has strengths and distinct challenges compared to many other people. For me, being autistic means I interact with the world in ways that are different than other people. These differences manifest as strengths and struggles. Being autistic makes me who I am, and I like who I am.

Autistic individuals face significant challenges in a world

that is not designed for us, but by acknowledging the barriers and finding helpful accommodations we can mitigate those difficulties. However, it is important for allistic people to remember that we are not defined solely by the struggles that come with being autistic. We possess unique strengths that contribute to our identities. These strengths might include exceptional verbal or visual memory, advanced problem-solving skills, active listening abilities, culinary talents, artistic skills, or extensive knowledge in a particular area of interest. Our remarkable attributes and talents are just as much a part of our identities as our struggles—even more so. By recognizing and celebrating our capabilities, allistic people can make room for our valuable contributions to the world. This truth is empowering for autistic individuals.

Forming a positive identity can be challenging if autistic people primarily see themselves as a collection of struggles and deficits. What may be perceived as weaknesses in the *Diagnostic and Statistical Manual of Mental Disorders* should be seen as strengths. By reframing the way we think about autism, we can shift how we view autistic individuals.

For example, instead of saying that autistic people demonstrate *differences in social communication,* we can say that autistic people are great at *honest and direct communication.* Instead of describing autistic people as being *fixated on a narrow range of interests,* we can say that they have *a profound and extensive base of knowledge.* Rather than saying autistic people *lack interest in socializing with people,* we can say that they *give highly focused attention to each person.* And instead of referring to an autistic person's *adherence to routine,* we can point out that the person is *incredibly stable, consistent, and trustworthy,* which are all beneficial in personal and professional

Identity

contexts.

This type of reframing can help autistic people build a positive identity, and it can foster a greater understanding and appreciation of the diverse ways autistic individuals contribute to society. By recognizing these strengths, we can better support and celebrate each person's unique qualities.

The world is gradually shifting its perspective on autism, but such changes take time. During this transition period, it is crucial to remember that differences are not deficits. We can continue to encourage and promote positive change while also nurturing our own identities and well-being. It is easy to become overwhelmed by negative thoughts, especially when external voices perpetuate and reinforce negative perceptions of autism. Therefore, we should focus on our strengths and the positive aspects of our identities. In these ways, we can foster a supportive environment for ourselves and others in the autistic community.

You Are Not Static

Because identity formation is a life-long process full of new experiences and change, I have found it helpful to keep a journal. I write about my feelings and experiences as I try new things. Reflecting on these entries has provided insights into what has truly resonated with me over time, which helps me to build a more authentic identity and to rely less on a mask. The journey is ongoing, but each step forward brings more clarity and confidence.

I did not feel like I was getting to know myself until age twenty-three. At that point, I went through a period of grief, reflecting on what might have been different if I had gained a better knowledge of myself earlier in life. Perhaps I would have had more support. Maybe I would not have had to endure so much bullying, or face so many learning struggles, or struggle with such poor mental health. (For this reason, I am a strong advocate for early diagnosis.) Thankfully, I have reached a place of peace. I have accepted myself for who I am. Understanding and accepting my autism allowed me to reframe my past experiences, viewing them through a lens of compassion rather than regret.

As an autistic person begins to live more authentically, allistic people might notice significant changes in that person. Allistic people might assume that an autistic friend or coworker is becoming "more autistic." However, those allistic people are witnessing an autistic person who is no longer camouflaging and who is discovering a true expression of the self.

This is why autistic people need support from understanding friends, family, and communities. This relational network can provide the encouragement and validation that autistic people need to unmask and explore their identities. Online and offline communities of autistic individuals can offer invaluable support and shared experiences, helping them feel less alone.

Your identity is not static; it will continue to evolve as you grow and learn more about yourself. Embrace the changes and be patient with yourself. The process of unmasking and self-discovery is ongoing. Take it one step at a time. Each small step towards authenticity is a victory.

CHAPTER 3

Sensory Experiences

The information we receive through our senses significantly influences how we interact with our environments and process stimuli. For instance, certain tastes might be perceived as toxic, leading us to avoid ingesting them, or specific sound frequencies may cause pain, prompting us to steer clear of them. These sensory perceptions shape our behaviors and choices.

Some autistic individuals require support to manage and enhance sensory experiences. This support can help them remain regulated and able to fully engage with their surroundings. Autistic people benefit from tools, accommodations, and tailored strategies that help them adapt to each situation. The toolkit, or what we might call a "Swiss Army knife," might include things like noise-cancelling headphones and fidget spinners.

Autistic individuals' sensory experiences are usually different than those of allistic people. These differences might be related to taste, smell, touch, vision, hearing, balance (vestibular), body awareness (proprioception), or internal body sensations (interoception). Each autistic person's sensory experiences can vary widely compared to other autistic people. Some might be *hyposensitive,* meaning they require more stimulation to feel regulated. Think of hyposensitivity as a constant desire for more extra-strong coffee. Hyposensitive individuals, also known as sensory seekers, actively search for sensory input. Others may be *hypersensitive,* which means they need less stimulation. These people might find that even minimal sensory input is overwhelming or painful. Every background noise could feel like a painful rock concert in the person's head.

Some people are hypersensitive in relation to one stimulus and hyposensitive in response to another. For example, someone might be hypersensitive to noise but hyposensitive to visual stimuli. The same person might use noise-cancelling headphones when working and then enjoy watching strobe lights. These variations reflect the distinct sensory profile of each person, which highlights the need for personalized approaches to sensory regulation and support. Understanding these profiles can help tailor environments and strategies to meet the unique needs of autistic individuals.

Taste

Eating and cooking food does not only involve taste, of course. All the senses can be involved when we prepare and enjoy meals. Autistic people do not experience taste in isolation from the other senses, but for the sake of simplicity, I will only focus on taste in my discussion here.

Many autistic individuals have strong food preferences and avoidances. As a result, they often prefer what is known as the "beige diet," which consists of foods like crisps, chocolate, biscuits, white bread, pasta, and chicken nuggets. Comfort food at its finest! The beige diet typically excludes colorful fruits and vegetables. Fruits and vegetables have many flavors, which means that each bite is unpredictable. By contrast, foods like chocolate offer a consistent taste with every bite. Thus, a beige diet reduces the sensory stimuli an autistic person encounters, making it a more appealing choice.

The consistent taste and texture of beige diet foods can provide a sense of comfort and predictability, which is important for hypersensitive autistic individuals. The lack of strong or unpredictable flavors in the beige diet can help prevent sensory overload. (I have never heard someone complain that a chicken nugget is too spicy or that a biscuit is too sour.) The beige diet might seem bland to some people, but it is a deliciously predictable experience of comfort for others.

When I was a child, my diet was very restricted. I often ate little or no breakfast. I would not eat during the day. I only ate some food at dinner, depending on what it was. I could go twenty-four hours without eating, if nothing seemed appealing or comfortable. You can imagine how such behavior might be worrisome for parents. In these cases, parents are often instructed not to worry and to allow the autistic child to eat when so desired. The idea is that the child will eventually eat before starving. However, this view can be dangerous. Autistic people sometimes have difficulty feeling hunger, so they need reminders to eat. Throughout primary school, I often felt sick around lunchtime because I lacked proper nutrition, which prevented me from fully engaging in afternoon classes. My mother, concerned about my eating habits, sought advice from a friend who had an anorexic child. Her friend suggested that it did not matter what I ate as long as I was eating *something*.

Helen, due to her food sensitivities, also has a very limited diet. She often sticks to a small number of familiar, safe, and tolerable foods. People sometimes pressure her to try new foods or they criticize her diet. That makes eating a difficult and shameful experience, which in turn encourages her to avoid food altogether.

Autistic people should be allowed to enjoy their preferred

foods. Doing so will reduce anxiety about eating and ensure that something is consumed. If chicken nuggets and biscuits are the go-to, let them be the go-to. By providing a sense of comfort and security with familiar foods, the overall stress about meals can be greatly reduced, promoting better nutrition and emotional well-being in the long run.

Taste, for all people, is a crucial sense for ingestive behavior. However, an estimated 90 percent of autistic children have difficulties with taste. Autistic people can struggle to identify certain flavors, such as citric acid, which affects their perception of food and therefore food preferences. For example, citric acid is found in foods like lemons, limes, pineapples, tomatoes, broccoli, and other fruits and vegetables. So, it is easy to see why sensory difficulties in this area would lead to health concerns such as weight loss or gain, or illnesses. Difficulty identifying tastes may lead to food refusal (being extremely "picky") or to a strong fear of trying new foods.

I always ask about the ingredients in a meal before eating it. I want to avoid surprises and to know exactly what flavors to expect. If I am told something vague like, "You will see," then eating becomes a less pleasurable, anxiety-inducing experience. Autistic people prefer descriptions like, "It's sweet and crunchy" or "It's savory with a hint of basil." Specific descriptions can transform the dining experience from nerve-wracking to delightful. My mother has always been good at explaining the taste of each food. Her approach greatly reduces anxiety and helps me feel more comfortable with trying new foods. Therefore, caregivers, friends, and family members should strive to provide autistic people with transparent, detailed descriptions.

When trying new foods, I find it helpful to ask someone to taste the food first and describe it to me. That helps me determine

Sensory Experiences

whether the food is "Phoebe-friendly." Sam finds the "food expansion" method to be helpful. The idea is to place a new type of food near the autistic person without any pressure to eat it, which is like letting the food "join the party" without making it the center of attention. After a few days or weeks, an autistic person might be willing to touch it or to allow new types of food to be on the plate. Eventually, the person might try a bite. Whatever the case, the autistic person should have freedom to explore the option or reject it.

This method acknowledges the sensory differences and anxieties that often accompany the food experiences of autistic individuals, and it provides a structured yet flexible approach to expanding the diet. I am more likely to try a new food after I have seen it being prepared, watched other people eating it, and discussed with those people what it was like. Bon appétit! One step at a time!

If you have dietary concerns about yourself, a friend, or a child, it is essential to seek advice from a qualified medical professional. Consulting a nutritionist, occupational therapist, or general practitioner can provide tailored guidance to address specific needs and challenges.

Smell

Research has shown that autistic people use different areas of the brain to process scents than allistic people. Autistic people often experience aromas more intensely. The way they perceive aromas depends on whether they are hyposensitive or hypersensitive. The former often seek to experience strong scents, such as incense, candles, and curry powder. They may also be drawn to comforting scents, such as those associated with familiar people. For example, smelling the hair or skin of a familiar person can bring joy, comfort, or calm to autistic people. By contrast, hypersensitive people can feel overwhelmed by strong aromas. Common items like air fresheners or cooking smells can trigger sensory overload.

Autistic individuals often possess an enhanced sense of smell. They can detect nuances that allistic individuals might miss. It is important to help autistic people if they say they are struggling with strong or unusual smells. Without help, they might increase stimming to cope with sensory overload, or they might find it hard to concentrate, or they might experience a meltdown (more about those in chapter 4).

Helen describes herself as having a heightened sensitivity to smell, often detecting scents that others might not notice. This can make environments overwhelming for her if there are strong or unusual odors, such as perfumes, cleaning chemicals, or garbage. Pleasant scents like fresh flowers or baking bread can be very comforting for her. For Helen, smells can significantly impact her mood and concentration. Pleasant scents can help her feel calm and focused, creating a sense of well-being. On the other hand, unpleasant odors can cause anxiety, distraction, or even headaches and nausea.

Allistic people can support their autistic friends and family members by using fragrance-free products, avoiding candles or incense, providing foods that suit the senses, and minimizing exposure to distressing smells. Ensuring good ventilation in living spaces can help. I often seek out pleasant smells for their calming effects. I have multiple candles in every room and enjoy the scents

Sensory Experiences

of my comfort people. But I also experience sensory overload when confronted with an abundance of scents. When too many aromas bombard my senses, my brain struggles to process them all. So, it is important to understand and respect each autistic person's specific aroma triggers.

Touch

When people think about the tactile sense, they often imagine one person reaching out to touch another. However, this sense also encompasses the feeling of materials, the texture of food, and the weight or pressure of objects. Consequently, it impacts many areas of our lives, from the clothes we wear to the food we eat to the experiences we have with surfaces.

The tactile sense can be a source of pleasure and discomfort. For example, some autistic individuals might seek out certain textures that feel soothing, such as soft fabrics or weighted blankets, while avoiding others that cause distress, like scratchy clothing or sticky substances. This sensitivity to touch can influence daily activities, including dressing, eating, and engaging in physical activities.

Autistic individuals frequently dislike "light touching" and prefer a firmer touch. For instance, some autistic people might prefer tight squeezes more than light hugs. Others might find light hair brushing uncomfortable. Some autistic people avoid casual physical contact altogether. When someone engages in casual physical contact with me, such as lightly resting a hand on my arm, back, or leg, I remove the person's hand and firmly brush over the touched area. Until I do this, which is like pressing a reset button for my skin, I cannot continue with any activity or conversation. But when I do that, the other person might understandably take offense. When I was younger, I could not provide a comprehensive explanation for my behavior or assure the other person that my actions were not a sign of dislike. Now that I can explain the reason for my reaction, the people who are close to me understand and engage in firmer touches, squeezes, and hugs. Their willingness to adapt to my needs helps me feel more comfortable and connected with them.

I have often heard the argument that touch is essential for forming social bonds. The belief is that hugging, holding hands, and casual social contact help develop friendships, relationships, and familial ties. However, if someone is uncomfortable being hugged, that expression will not form a positive relationship; instead, hugging might be associated with negative feelings about the other person.

There are many ways other than physical contact to bond with autistic people. One way to strengthen relational bonds is through shared time and activities. Another way is through communication, especially by listening with respect. If the autistic person prefers firm touches and no surprise contact, it is best to ask for permission before hugging, and then it is usually best to provide a firm bear hug. If the autistic person prefers to initiate contact, it is best to wait respectfully.

Helen finds physical contact, like hugs or handshakes, to be overwhelming, especially if it is unexpected. She appreciates physical affection from close family members and friends, but she prefers to initiate the contact or at least be prepared for it. Unexpected touches can be jarring and uncomfortable. In all cases, communication, understanding, and respect is vital. Respecting these preferences

Sensory Experiences

fosters positive and meaningful connections.

I hate having anything touch my feet. I always wear socks inside and shoes outside. My feet have a very strict "no touch" policy that is enforced every day of the week. However, for those who enjoy feeling textures with their feet, several strategies can enhance the benefits of being barefoot. One effective method is "ground time." This involves finding an outdoor area with grass, sand, soil, or any other safe natural surface and then standing or walking while focusing on the textures of the surface. Another strategy involves standing near a wall for balance, placing a tennis ball under one foot, and rolling the ball around under the bare foot. It is like a foot massage! These activities can help some autistic people enhance sensory experiences and promote emotional relaxation and grounding. That is not true for me. I prefer my feet to be encased in my trusty socks and shoes. I cannot stand the thought of having my bare feet on anything!

A stereotypical autistic trait, frequently depicted in books and movies, is the need to cut off clothing labels. Based on my experiences and those of other autistic individuals, this is often true. Many of us face an ongoing battle with clothing labels. Imagine having an itch you cannot reach, such as when wearing a cast for a broken arm. Now imagine that the itch is all-consuming, invading your brain and taking over your body. Clothing labels are like that. You become so focused on the scratchy, irritating label that is rubbing the back of your neck that you cannot think about anything else. It *must go*. I can get so frustrated with a label that I rip it off, which has caused several holes in my shirts. I have sacrificed many shirts in the Great Label Wars. So, I recommend using a small seam ripper. That tool will help you avoid clothing casualties in your war against labels. You can also try to buy sensory-friendly clothing from online stores that offer clothes without irritating labels. These stores also offer a variety of materials designed to help people with sensory needs. If you ever find yourself in the throes of label-induced madness, remember that there are ways to achieve victory without sacrificing your wardrobe.

When purchasing clothing, consider these questions to ensure you feel comfortable and confident in your choices. Will the fabric, hooks, zippers, and buttons feel good against your skin? Will you be able to sit down, stand up, and move your arms freely and comfortably in this clothing? Is it easy to put on and take off? Does the clothing allow for temperature regulation?

An autistic person's sensory preferences can change depending on the circumstances. When I am overwhelmed by my environment, I need to reduce sensory input. In these cases, I use a blanket that I named Rupert. I love Rupert very much. He is soft and cuddly, and I often wear him around my neck like a cape. I bring him with me to most places. Everyone in my life knows about my attachment to him. However, there are rare occasions when I cannot stand anything touching me, including Rupert. At one moment I might be cuddled up with Rupert and then suddenly I must throw him across the room. My friend finds this extremely amusing, but Rupert does not take offense. Unfortunately, the same type of sudden change can happen in my interactions with people, which might cause them to take offense. I might be holding a friend's hand and then suddenly need to let go. Thankfully, my friends understand and do not feel offended.

I wrote earlier about the taste of food, but the *texture* of food also plays a role in an autistic person's eating habits. Some prefer crunchy foods and others prefer mushy or smooth foods. Emma cannot stand soft food, but I love soft foods. I usually mash everything before eating. As a child, I often got into trouble for mashing my cake into chocolate mush. Apparently "cake soup" was not on the menu. Nowadays, I horrify my friend by microwaving nacho chips to make them soft. Culinary sacrilege!

Autistic individuals might find it hard to eat foods that do not fit with their preferred texture. When the texture (or smell) of a food is wrong, I gag and dry heave—a spontaneous reaction that I cannot avoid. I have learned to adapt my meals to suit my sensory needs. So, you should not berate autistic people for "playing with their food" or accuse them of being rude. They are doing what is necessary to get food into their body, and that is a positive thing. It is important to respect and support each person's sensory preferences to ensure a comfortable and positive eating experience. After all, everyone has their quirks; some of us just happen to have a refined culinary preference for microwave-softened nachos.

Vision

Depending on whether they are hyposensitive or hypersensitive, autistic individuals may either seek out intense visual stimulation or avoid it. Visual stimulation can come from bright, flashing, or fluorescent lights, or from "visual clutter," which occurs when an environment is filled with items of all types and shapes scattered across the floor, desks, tables, and cupboards. Visual clutter can overstimulate autistic people, making it hard for them to effectively accomplish tasks. I often found this challenging in classrooms, which were cluttered with posters, seats, paint, bright lights, collages, and colored whiteboard pens.

When autistic people try to process all the information from this type of clutter, they struggle to focus. Overstimulation makes it difficult for them to learn in class, clean a room, or shop at the supermarket. Reducing visual clutter helps autistic individuals to engage in and complete tasks. Creating an environment with minimal visual clutter can significantly enhance their ability to concentrate and perform effectively.

Just as we all need a healthy natural environment with clean air and water, autistic people also need environments designed for their well-being. The Prospect and Refuge Theory explains why people need to feel secure within their environment and why certain settings meet this need. *Prospect* refers to the need to preview and understand one's environment to ensure it meets the person's needs. *Refuge* describes the ability to seek protection or safety from sensory stimulation within the environment. This can be challenging for autistic individuals if the visual clutter continuously changes, especially without warning. For example, in a classroom, furniture might be rearranged, new items might be introduced, new posters might be hung, and the whiteboard might be frequently moved. Ever-changing visual clutter can be so overwhelming that we are unable to preview our environment before entering, causing us to immediately seek refuge to escape the sensory overload. That behavior can include elopement (running away), meltdowns, shutdowns, or stimming. Ensuring a stable and predictable environment with minimal visual changes can help autistic individuals feel more secure and reduce the likelihood of these responses. Creating consistent and organized spaces can significantly enhance our ability to process the surroundings and participate effectively.

Research indicates that autistic individuals often have greater peripheral vision than allistic people. Consequently, they must exert more energy to focus on what is directly in front of them. When an environment is visually cluttered, autistic people can find it challenging to ignore the peripheral stimuli, which leads to sensory overload. That overload can significantly impede our ability to concentrate on the task at hand.

Driving can be challenging for me because there is an abundance of visual stimuli, such as cars, lights, people, and shops. I feel like I am trying to drive through a neon jungle! Bright moving elements, such as cars, are especially difficult to process. Driving at night is even more overwhelming because there are so many moving lights. Despite all these factors, I am still able to focus on driving, remember road rules, navigate to my destination, and think about other things like the scripts I will use during conversations upon arrival. But my anxiety increases significantly. My friends understand this experience, so they usually do not ask me to drive at night. During the day, I try to avoid driving on unfamiliar routes or during busy times. I have become an experienced "passenger princess," which means I get to enjoy the ride without the stress of driving, and I get to control the music, which is a perk no one should underestimate. This arrangement helps me manage my anxiety and ensures that I arrive at my destination without feeling like I have just run a sensory marathon. I may not be behind the wheel, but I can fully control my comfort and well-being.

Anxiety and feeling overwhelmed can be alleviated if allistic people provide pictures of new environments before autistic people enter those spaces. This way autistic people can prepare for what they will encounter. In addition, allistic friends and colleagues can ensure that a location has a refuge where autistic people can escape sensory stimulation. This could be a designated area in a classroom or a room in a house. These areas, often referred to as "sensory-friendly zones," are most effective when chosen in collaboration with the autistic person. This ensures that the space meets that person's specific needs, which can significantly enhance comfort and the ability to cope with sensory overload.

To reduce overstimulation caused by bright, flashing, or fluorescent lights, it helps to use warmer lightbulbs, a dimmer switch, or lamps instead of overhead lights. My friends can tell when the lights are affecting me because I blink more frequently and each blink is longer and more forceful, like I am trying to signal something in Morse code. (SOS: Save Our Senses!) On one occasion, our kitchen light was flickering, turning the room into an unintentional disco club and causing me significant distress. My father promptly climbed onto the kitchen bench and removed the bulb, ending the unwanted panic! If indoor bright lights are overstimulating, it can help to wear sunglasses. Allistic people should respect this choice because it can help autistic people to comfortably engage with their surroundings.

An environment that does not cause sensory overload allows autistic people to make one of their best contributions: attention to detail. When I was younger, I aspired to be an editor because I loved combing through text for grammatical errors and spelling mistakes. Nothing like the thrill of catching a rogue comma! I also dreamed of becoming a teacher because I enjoyed marking the fine details of homework. Reducing visual stimulation allows me to concentrate on small details even better, and that enables me to notice patterns that others might miss. This skill enhances my research, writing, and hobbies, bringing me immense joy. It is amazing what I can achieve when my environment is not screaming for my attention.

Some autistic people want to be surrounded by bright lights or visual clutter. These individuals derive pleasure and experience better self-regulation through increased visual stimulation. They might enjoy using diversely colored light bulbs, adorning their surroundings with posters, and setting up decorative objects throughout the living space. When the environment is tailored to their preferences, they can engage more effectively in their tasks and experience a sense of safety and contentment.

Hearing

Sensitivity to sound is a widely discussed aspect of autism because many autistic individuals experience adverse reactions to the sounds around them. This condition, known as *hyperacusis,* is defined as a decreased tolerance to environmental sounds. Certain sounds may be particularly intolerable, such as loud horns; multiple noises occurring simultaneously, such as group conversations; high-pitched noises, like sirens; and prolonged noises, such as the constant hum of fans. These sounds can cause intense irritation, distraction, anxiety, and even pain. The impact of hyperacusis can be profound, affecting an autistic person's ability to engage in social interactions.

Autistic individuals often describe everyday sounds, such as hairdryers or fans, as painful and overwhelming. Even a small computer fan can overwhelm my brain and reduce me to tears. The noise becomes so intrusive that I can no longer focus on anything else; it feels almost like relentless torture. I have noticed that allistic people are generally unaffected by these sounds, which highlights the stark difference in the ways that autistic individuals experience auditory stimuli.

Allistic people generally experience *habituation,* which is when someone gets used to a stimulus the more it is presented to them. Therefore, when allistic people hear a sound multiple times or for a prolonged period, they likely become habituated to it. Their psychological responses to the sound decrease as it fades into the background of their mind. Autistic people often do not have this luxury. Many autistic individuals are unable to become accustomed to certain stimuli, or habituation may take much longer than it does for allistic people. Instead, autistic people tend to experience the opposite of habituation, which is sensory overload. During these instances, autistic individuals may go through a meltdown or shutdown as a way to cope. (I explain more about these two reactions in chapter 4.)

I often experience shutdowns when dealing with auditory overload, causing me to withdraw. This is the best way for me to manage the intense pressure in my brain. In these moments, my brain is like a computer that is overloaded with too much information. On a computer, the "rainbow wheel of death" appears and it will not function until it processes the information. The same thing happens with my brain. When I am overloaded, my mental wheel of death pops up and I become unable to think, talk, or move until I have processed the information. If only Ctrl+Alt+Del worked on brains! This type of shutdown is my brain's way of protecting itself from a more severe overload, giving me the time and space to recover from the overwhelming sensory input. My brain goes into safe mode. Instead of tech support, I need peace and quiet.

In these situations, the most effective remedy for me is to

Sensory Experiences

distance myself from or shut off the auditory input. This might involve swiftly exiting a supermarket, suddenly turning off the TV, or putting on my noise-cancelling headphones. I often receive support from my friends and family. They help me leave overwhelming events, or they reduce the auditory stimuli in an environment, or they help me become mentally prepared for places that might trigger a shutdown. They also allow me to wear my headphones without criticism. By offering this support, they help create an inclusive and comfortable environment where I can function effectively. I am often unaware of the onset of auditory overload, but my friends have become attuned to my behavior and can alert me when they think I am close to the edge. I am very thankful for their assistance.

I and other autistic individuals who struggle with sound sensitivities react to sensory overload situations in common ways. These behaviors include covering our ears, crying, avoiding sound, exhibiting a tense or shaky body, increased pace of breathing, more stimming and humming. Recognizing these signs early can be crucial for timely intervention and support, thereby preventing a meltdown or shutdown.

I often hum or make other vocalizations throughout the day. By focusing on my own sounds, I focus less on the painful and distracting external ones. This self-regulatory strategy allows me to create a more manageable auditory environment. It also helps me to hold my breath when I or someone nearby needs to make a loud noise, such as using a blender. When warned about the impending noise, I hold my breath to create additional pressure within my body, which helps me feel more regulated. This tactic is particularly useful when my hands are occupied. However, I only use this strategy for about four seconds at a time, ensuring I never put myself in any danger. I do not recommend using this strategy for more than a few seconds. There are also other ways to manage auditory overload and maintain a sense of control over one's sensory environment.

Autistic individuals often struggle to distinguish between diverse sounds, which makes it challenging to prioritize the sounds we hear. For instance, if there is a siren in the distance, three conversations happening in the same room, music playing from a sound system, and a baby crying, the autistic person might pay attention to all these sounds at once. This overwhelming sensory experience can lead to significant stress and anxiety. These difficulties make it hard for autistic people to focus on a single auditory source in environments that are saturated with sounds, such as a shopping mall or supermarket. This can be detrimental to relationships during social interactions.

I struggle when someone is talking to me while other conversations are happening around us or music is playing. I cannot prioritize a single voice, and that means that I do not retain any information from the conversation. At work, when someone wants to discuss something with me, I ask if we can move to a quieter room. This adjustment makes it much easier for me to perform my job effectively.

When surrounded by many sounds, I start to dissociate. All the sounds blur into one, like a swarm of bees in my head. It feels like I am drowning in endless waves of noise. All the sound blends into one din, like being submerged in a sea. My vision blurs. I feel disconnected from my body. I cannot move. This experience is incredibly draining, so it takes a long time for me to recover. During these situations, friends and family members help me find a safe, quiet space where I can begin to regulate and recuperate.

Sensory Experiences

Nevertheless, these situations can have a profound psychological effect, leading to fear of what might happen in the future. People naturally fear things that cause them pain. For autistic individuals, the experience of painful sounds can lead them to avoid social gatherings, grocery shopping, or sports and hobbies. Fear can significantly impact their quality of life, limiting opportunities for social interaction, physical activity, and enjoyment. Over time, this pattern of avoidance can contribute to feelings of isolation, which exacerbates anxiety and depression.

There are ways to help autistic individuals reduce negative auditory experiences. Allistic friends, coworkers, and family members can provide warnings about the potential for difficult auditory environments ahead of time. For example, if someone needs to use a food blender, that person can warn the autistic person beforehand. Then the autistic person can prepare, perhaps by going to a different location or putting on headphones. Allistic people can also establish a designated safe area where the autistic person can regain composure. This space can be used for stimming, wearing noise-cancelling headphones, or using other self-regulation methods. Knowing there is a safe retreat can reduce anxiety and make it easier to participate in activities.

There are also things that autistic people can do to help themselves. Each of us is unique, but some people benefit from deep pressure techniques. Some employ sensory tools like headphones, or they establish routines that reduce negative auditory experiences. Autistic people can also preestablish an exit plan before they attend social or professional events, which can increase confidence during unknown situations. The exit plan might include ways to communicate with colleagues and friends, so that they know how to help when needed. There could be a discreet code sign, like tapping or squeezing a pinky finger, to indicate when the autistic person is feeling anxious. Knowing there is a preplanned way to leave if needed can make participating in events more feasible and less daunting.

Elevated noise sensitivity is not all bad. My heightened sensitivity means I have excellent hearing. My brain does not allow sounds to fade into the background. This enables me to notice subtle changes in sounds and hear conversations around me. While I was growing up, one of my parents' nicknames for me was "Bat Ears" because no matter where they were in the house, even if they were speaking quietly, I could hear their conversations and respond with quips and jokes. Imagine their surprise when, on one occasion, they were discussing secret birthday plans and I chimed in from two rooms away with, "I prefer chocolate cake!" My hearing capacity has led to many entertaining situations, so I have embraced my "Bat Ears" nickname. I can pick up important details in conversations or notice subtle changes in the environment that others might miss.

Vestibular

The vestibular sense is often overlooked because it is not one of the traditional five senses (taste, touch, hear, see, smell). But it is vital in life. Located in the inner ear, it plays a crucial role in balance and movement. This sense is fundamental to motor development, posture, eye movements, visual processing, and spatial awareness, such as depth perception. The intricate vestibular system influences how we perceive and control the speed and direction of our

Sensory Experiences

movements in relation to the environment.

Autistic people with hyposensitive vestibular systems have reduced sensitivity to motion stimuli, which leads them to actively seek opportunities for movement. They might display high levels of energy, frequently engaging in activities like running, climbing, spinning, and jumping (even from significant heights).They might enjoy playground equipment, Lycra fabric (for ease of movement), and wobbly egg chairs. Individuals with hyposensitive vestibular senses often enjoy making hammocks in which they can swing. This provides a heightened sensory experience for their vestibular system.

Because they love movement, autistic people with a hyposensitive vestibular sense might engage in dangerous behaviors as a means of self-regulation. They might be inclined to jump from extreme heights or run extremely long distances. Jumping from high places obviously poses significant risks. Running is healthy, but long-distance running solely to fulfill the need for intense vestibular stimulation can present hazards, particularly if the autistic individual wanders into unsafe environments, such as traffic, or into unfamiliar locations where it would be easy to get lost. Therefore, it is crucial for autistic and allistic individuals to familiarize themselves with safety guidelines. To mitigate risks, allistic and autistic people can create safe, structured opportunities for movement. For instance, parents can take children to supervised playgrounds, trampoline parks, or set up safe and fun equipment at home.

Autistic individuals with hypersensitive vestibular systems tend to be excessively reactive to movement stimuli. Heightened sensitivity to motion might manifest as clumsiness or lack of coordination, particularly when executing quick movements. Rapid actions can disrupt the body's equilibrium, resulting in, for example, an awkward walk. The way I walk might resemble a duck-like waddle because I am trying to regain balance. Picture a very determined, yet slightly tipsy duck navigating through a crowded room. My struggle to accurately process visual cues compounds my difficulties with spatial awareness. I frequently collide with walls, doors, objects, and people. Maintaining my balance is challenging, so I sometimes stumble or fall, which can surprise onlookers. Just the other day, I walked into a wall, ricocheted into the side of the bed, unsuccessfully tried to regain my balance, bounced into the wall again, knocked a framed picture to the floor, and fell. It was like a slapstick comedy routine, minus the laugh track.

Many autistic people have been described as having a gait that is wooden, robotic, stiff, or uncoordinated. My gait is paradoxically described as both bouncy and wooden. I frequently feel off balance while walking and often find myself instinctively reaching out with my hands to maintain stability. My parents say that I "walk by feel." We have humorously dubbed my posture as "T-Rex arms." Dancing with gravity is part of my normal daily life, but I have learned to navigate it with humor and resilience.

For individuals with hypersensitive vestibular senses, effective regulation techniques may involve gentle rocking or swinging. Items such as hammocks, sensory swings, and Swiss balls can serve as beneficial sensory tools. These tools provide soothing vestibular input that can help autistic individuals regain a sense of equilibrium. Engaging in these activities in a safe, controlled environment can significantly enhance our ability to process vestibular input without risk of injury.

Another potential strategy to support the vestibular sense (and potentially other senses such as proprioception) is to practice yoga.

Sensory Experiences

This activity can enhance balance, coordination, and overall sensory integration. Three fundamental poses can be particularly beneficial: the mountain pose, the cat pose, and the tree pose. The mountain pose is a standing pose that improves core strength and posture while promoting stability and alignment. The cat pose involves a gentle stretch, improving flexibility and posture. The tree pose is excellent for enhancing balance and focus because it requires maintaining equilibrium on one leg while engaging core muscles. Incorporating yoga poses into a regular routine can strengthen the vestibular sense, improve body awareness, and contribute to overall well-being.

It is also easy to find safe sensory tools, such as supervised playground equipment, hammocks, egg chairs, swings, and Swiss balls. It is important for allistic people and autistic people to discuss and establish safety parameters for individuals who might be inclined to engage in potentially dangerous behaviors, such as jumping from high places or running extremely long distances.

Proprioception

The proprioceptive system, located in our joints and muscles, plays a crucial role in our body's awareness of its positions and movements. The nervous system sends messages about these areas to our brain, informing us about our body's position relative to the surrounding environment. This sense plays a role in spatial awareness and coordination, providing essential information on how to navigate surroundings and how much force or pressure to apply in various tasks. For instance, when walking through a doorway, our proprioceptive system helps us move through the space without bumping into the doorframe. Similarly, when cracking an egg, this system helps us use the precise amount of force needed to break the shell without causing it to shatter excessively. As you can see, this system is vital for everyday activities.

Like other senses, autistic individuals can be either hypersensitive or hyposensitive to proprioceptive input. Autistic individuals who are hypersensitive may struggle to process it effectively. Hypersensitivity might cause them to exhibit unusual postures or positions. Such people often have difficulty staying still, so they sometimes purposefully crash into other people and objects to receive sensory input. Therefore, it can help to provide autistic people with short movement breaks, especially when prolonged sitting is expected. These breaks can involve activities like running, jumping, or climbing. Additionally, deep pressure techniques, such as using weighted blankets or giving tight bear hugs, can help meet the sensory needs of someone who needs proprioceptive input. Sensory tools like compression clothing can help individuals feel grounded and secure.

Autistic individuals who are hyposensitive to proprioceptive input often have a low awareness of their body's position in space. Their posture might appear floppy. They frequently lean on furniture, walls, or other people, in part because they might misjudge the personal space of others. It is like living in a perpetual pinball game, with the autistic person being the ball. This occurs because the proprioceptive system inaccurately measures the distance between one person and another. I often lean on my friends, especially when standing, because my body feels floppy and disorganized. This challenge is exacerbated when I am carrying something, such as a laundry basket. My proprioceptive sense does not adjust to include

Sensory Experiences

the basket, so I bump into more things.

Thankfully, there are solutions for helping people who struggle with the proprioceptive system. For example, I find deep pressure to be extremely calming and grounding, enhancing my body awareness. Deep pressure input can come from squeezes (best on hands or feet), bear hugs, or weighted blankets. Another option is to wear compression clothing, which provides constant pressure. Beyond pressure, it also helps to use squeezy stress balls, chewable jewelry (*chewelry*), and tangle cushions. I also enjoy sitting on my feet or in other positions where my body is contorted, providing constant pressure. These activities help me maintain a sense of calm and stability throughout the day.

I like carrying a squeezy stress ball to receive proprioceptive input on the go. Moving around at work or at the supermarket with a weighted blanket would not be convenient, but a squeezy stress ball can easily fit in pockets and bags. I always have one in my bag, and I keep them scattered throughout my house. This allows me to access proprioceptive input whenever I need it.

Chewelry offers a safe and effective way to receive proprioceptive input, which can be particularly helpful for individuals who, like me, might bite their tongue, cheeks, hands, or nails. These habits can cause physical damage and are difficult to explain to others, especially as a child. Chewelry comes in various forms, such as rings, necklaces, and bracelets, with different bite strengths, shapes, colors, sizes, and textures to meet individual needs. For more discreet options, there are pencil toppers or chew tags that can be used at school or on the go. Chewing gum can also help.

Trampolines offer a fun way to get proprioceptive input through dynamic movement, enhancing body awareness and control. And occupational therapists can provide personalized guidance on a range of sensory equipment and exercises tailored to meet each person's unique needs.

Interoception

Interoception is the sense responsible for awareness and understanding of the body's internal signals. *Awareness* refers to recognizing internal signals or feelings, whereas *understanding* involves accurately interpreting what the signals indicate. People can have varying levels of accuracy and attentiveness in their interoceptive sense. Those with a highly attentive interoceptive sense are aware of their internal feelings but they might struggle to pinpoint exactly what they are experiencing. Conversely, those with a more accurate interoceptive sense may not notice every internal feeling but they can accurately identify and understand the ones they recognize. This distinction points to the complexity of interoception and its role in how we perceive and respond to internal bodily states. Understanding interoception can be crucial for improving overall well-being, because it affects everything from recognizing hunger and thirst to detecting emotional and physical discomfort.

Interoception is crucial for signaling our emotions and physical needs, such as fatigue, nausea, pain, or the need to use the bathroom. For some individuals, it is difficult to recognize these internal signals, which can make it hard to know when to eat, drink, or rest. When this sense does not function well, people have a harder time finding emotional and physical homeostasis. Therefore, developing and honing interoceptive skills can improve physical health and

Sensory Experiences

emotional regulation, leading to a more balanced and fulfilling life.

Variations in interoception can appear in several different ways. For example, some people have difficulty expressing, feeling, or correctly identifying emotions. This is known as *alexithymia,* which is very common among autistic individuals. In all people, emotions often cause physiological changes such as muscular tension, changes in heart rate, breathing patterns, tears, or smiling. Autistic people might struggle to accurately identify these physical changes and the corresponding emotions. This difficulty can lead to uncertainty about what we are feeling. For instance, if I notice an increased heart rate, it could mean that I am nervous, excited, or tired from exercise; or maybe I just saw a cute dog. Who knows? To better understand my emotional response to an increased heart rate, I need to consider my context. Sometimes I ask others about how they usually feel in similar situations. I often tell friends that I am feeling something and ask them to help me decipher what those feelings mean. It is like playing an emotional version of twenty questions, but I am trying to figure out whether I am excited or anxious, or if I just saw a cute dog. My board of trustees' support and insights often help me decode my feelings.

When I am not in tune with my emotions, I find it is much harder for me to process emotional situations or effectively communicate how I feel. This can lead to increased stress and anxiety, and feelings of being misunderstood and isolated. It is incredibly stressful when I know I am feeling something, but I cannot identify what it is. This creates communication barriers, especially during emotional disagreements or when making important decisions. It often takes me a week or two to process my emotions. By that time, most people have moved on from the discussion and decisions have already been made. Delayed emotional processing causes difficulties in social situations, deters me from participating in future engagements, and prevents me from expressing my feelings and needs at the proper time. All these outcomes further contribute to a sense of disconnection and isolation.

I often do not recognize an emotion until it becomes overwhelming. At that point, it becomes much harder to regulate. As I mentioned earlier, I am often unaware that I am becoming overwhelmed until I receive proprioceptive input and begin to regulate. Only then do I realize that I had been dysregulated. When I cannot understand why I feel a certain way, it is harder to express my needs to others. Do I feel overwhelmed because of a physical signal or because I have too many tasks to complete? When I cannot understand the reasons for my emotions, it is much harder to regulate them.

Allistic friends, coworkers, and family members can help by occasionally checking in to ask how the autistic person is doing. Sometimes allistic people can recognize when the autistic person is beginning to feel overwhelmed. As for self-care, autistic people can use grounding exercises to help them focus on their body and its sensations. One such exercise is the 5-4-3-2-1 method, which involves identifying five visible objects, four tactile objects, three sounds, two aromas, and one flavor. Another useful technique is deep breathing, which can help slow the heart rate and create a sense of calm. Grounding exercises, when practiced regularly, can enhance interoceptive awareness, making it easier to identify and manage emotions before they become overwhelming.

Interoception plays a crucial role in maintaining bodily homeostasis in relation to hunger and nutrition. The feeling of

Sensory Experiences

hunger prompts us to eat. However, this equilibrium is disrupted if we do not recognize the sensation of hunger. As mentioned earlier, I often do not feel hungry for extended periods. When I start feeling faint, I realize it is time to eat. For this reason, it helps when other people remind me to eat, albeit without mandatory wording. Being forced to eat can feel so unpleasant to an autistic person that it creates an unhealthy relationship with food. The best approach is for allistic people to offer kind and gentle eating prompts rather than pressure. Autistic people can also establish regular meal times and set alarms as reminders to eat before they experience extreme hunger or fainting episodes.

I use my friends as "body doubles" to help me eat. It is easier to consume food when others around me are also eating. Their presence provides the necessary support and motivation for me to eat, even if they are not directly interacting with me, which can make mealtimes more manageable and less overwhelming. For those who struggle with interoception, the social context and visual cues from others who are eating can serve as gentle reminders to eat. Sharing meals with friends or family can make eating a more enjoyable and less stressful experience while fostering a sense of connection and support.

Interoception also affects body states other than hunger, including hydration, sleep, temperature regulation, and pain. Autistic individuals often find it challenging to recognize when they are thirsty, which can lead to insufficient fluid intake. Considering that the human body is about 60 percent water, inadequate hydration can cause health issues such as headaches, dizziness, and digestive problems. To combat this, using drink bottles with motivational messages can serve as reminders to stay hydrated throughout the day. Trying flavored liquids can also encourage more frequent drinking. Additionally, setting alarms or reminders on a phone or other device can prompt regular drinking intervals. Establishing a routine or habit of drinking water at specific times, such as with meals or during breaks, can also help foster consistent hydration.

Autistic people frequently have difficulty recognizing that they are tired, which can result in staying up late and not getting enough sleep. Lack of sleep can negatively impact memory, digestion, mood, and energy levels. To improve sleep quality, it helps to establish a consistent nighttime routine with activities that signal it is time to wind down, such as drinking hot milk with honey and meditating before bed. Setting reminders or alarms can help maintain a consistent routine, ensuring that the body receives regular cues for sleep. Creating a calm environment in the bedroom, reducing screen time before bed, and engaging in relaxing activities like reading or listening to soothing music can further enhance the ability to fall and stay asleep.

Autistic individuals may struggle to recognize if they are hot or cold. I do not feel the cold as much as others. Once, while in Canada, I wore a sundress and flats in knee-deep snow, resulting in frostnip and a need for foil blankets. I looked like a confused (yet fashionable) snowman. Similarly, when I get too hot, I might not realize it until I feel faint. In either case, it takes a long time for my body to return to homeostasis. It helps me to observe what others are wearing. If people are wearing scarves, hats, and gloves, I realize that I should probably wear more than a sundress—unless I want to start a new trend called "fashionable frostbite."

I appreciate suggestions from friends and family members,

but I might not always want to listen when someone pushes me to wear a jacket. Phrasing suggestions in a nondemanding way is more effective. I prefer to hear a recommendation like this: "It is six degrees (Celsius) and raining outside. You may want a raincoat, or you may not. It's up to you." That allows me to make the decision without feeling pressured. Weather apps also help me to make informed choices about appropriate clothing.

Autistic individuals may have a very high pain threshold. That might seem advantageous, but it can be harmful. They might be unaware of injuries due to diminished pain signals, leading to delayed medical treatment for serious issues like appendicitis or broken bones.

Diminished pain signals can lead some autistic people to take unsafe risks, such as jumping from dangerous heights or using water that is too hot. The brain might not send a "danger" signal ahead of time. For this reason, it is important for autistic and allistic friends to discuss potentially unsafe situations. My friends remind me to stay approximately two meters away from the edge of a cliff, or to always wear an oven mitt when touching a hot dish. (Who knew that bare hands and hot dishes do not mix?) My friends are patient and kind when answering my questions about every potential danger, which enables me to avoid hazards and stay safe. Plus, it gives everyone plenty of opportunities to practice their "danger alert" faces when I get too close to the edge.

Interoception differences can affect all areas of physical and mental health—*simultaneously.* Put yourself in this scenario: You have not slept well because you went to bed late, but you do not feel tired. You have not eaten all day due to a lack of hunger signals, and you have not had any water because you did not feel thirsty.

You are not feeling well but you cannot pinpoint the reason. Some friends suggest that it might help to go outside, so you decide to go for a walk up a hill next to a cliff. On the path, despite feeling a little faint, you fearlessly walk close to the edge because your brain does not alert you to danger. This excursion might result in a dangerous fall or a fainting episode.

My point is that autistic people often struggle with a *combination of factors* that, taken as a whole, can be extremely overwhelming and dangerous. Allistic people need to understand the importance of helping autistic friends and coworkers manage interoceptive challenges. I share this not to seek pity but to help readers understand the challenges that many autistic people face. By increasing awareness, autistic people can better understand how to help ourselves and how to allow others to support us.

There are a few questions that autistic people and their allistic friends can use to better understand the specific needs. For example, some good discussion questions are: How aware are you of your body's internal signals, such as hunger, thirst, or the need to use the bathroom? Do you struggle to maintain regular eating or drinking habits, perhaps because it is difficult to recognize hunger or thirst? How do you ensure you get enough sleep? How do you know when you are feeling pain or illness. How do you incorporate interoceptive-friendly activities into your daily routine?

This chapter has delineated a spectrum of sensory experiences encountered by autistic individuals across the eight senses. People may experience hyposensitivity or hypersensitivity in different sensory domains. Therefore, it is important to craft a personalized approach for addressing individual sensory needs. Properly addressing sensory requirements will allow autistic individuals

Sensory Experiences

to focus on other aspects of life, such as work, education, social connections, and hobbies—all the elements of a full and well-rounded life.

It is hard to focus on mastering the latest dance moves or preparing a work presentation when you are distracted by scratchy clothing tags or blinding fluorescent lights. So, whether you prefer to tune out the world with noise-cancelling headphones or to find peace under a weighted blanket, remember that your sensory needs are just as important as anything else in your life.

CHAPTER 4

Meltdowns and Shutdowns

Many autistic individuals experience meltdowns, shutdowns, or both.

An autistic *meltdown* is an intense response to an overwhelming situation, triggered by factors such as sensory or social overload, changes, transitions, miscommunications, or a combination of these factors. Meltdowns occur when individuals are pushed beyond their ability to cope. A meltdown is not the same as a tantrum, which is usually a way for a person to manipulate a small audience. By contrast, meltdowns do not require an audience; they are not manipulative. Understanding this difference is crucial for providing appropriate support.

Autistic individuals often describe a meltdown as an overwhelming loss of control, which can result in crying, screaming, shouting, kicking, hitting, or biting. This can be frightening for those around the autistic person, but it is equally or more terrifying for the person who experiences it. Losing control of oneself is a deeply distressing experience. The person drowns in emotions and becomes unable to control actions or thoughts. This loss of control can lead to intense fear and panic, further exacerbating the meltdown. Many autistic people report feeling unable to breathe. Their thoughts become chaotic and they experience dissociation. Meltdowns can result in injury, so everyone should ensure the autistic person is in a safe space, away from crowds or potentially harmful objects.

Autistic individuals do not want to have meltdowns, so it is important for allistic friends, coworkers, and family members to respond with empathy and support. Each autistic person has unique needs during a meltdown, but there are strategies that can help. One is to reduce light and sound, and to minimize questions or talking. It might seem appropriate to ask an autistic person how you can help, but some questions can exacerbate the meltdown. Instead, it is more effective to create a calming environment and provide the person with a safe space to process emotions.

During a meltdown, autistic individuals may engage in harmful behaviors such as hair pulling, head banging, or scratching. These actions provide proprioceptive input, which can be calming and help them to regain control over their mind and body. However, there are safer ways to receive this input, such as using weighted blankets or receiving tight bear hugs.

Preparation is essential. Allistic people can work with the autistic person to develop a plan, which should be based on clear communication with the autistic person about what helps during meltdowns. Understanding the autistic person's preferences and triggers can guide allistic people toward providing effective and safe support. Here are some questions that can be used during the planning session. What triggers your meltdowns? What strategies help you during a meltdown? How do you recover from a meltdown? What steps are best to help you calm down and regain control? Are there any other ways that people around you can offer support during a meltdown?

When an autistic person is coming out of a meltdown, it is crucial to create a safe, judgment-free space. Meltdowns often

Meltdowns and Shutdowns

carry a stigma of being attention-seeking, which is untrue because autistic individuals cannot control their meltdowns. They are highly distressing for autistic people. Some describe feeling embarrassed afterward, especially if others witness the episode. Therefore, it is essential to show respect, kindness, empathy, love, and acceptance. In that type of reassuring relational context, autistic people feel secure and supported.

It may also be beneficial to provide a quiet, comfortable space where an autistic person can retreat and calm down without external pressures or distractions. Providing a soothing environment with minimal sensory input can aid the recovery. This space should be free from harsh lighting, loud noises, and other potential sensory triggers. Avoid bombarding the person with questions or attempting to immediately hold a discussion; instead, give the person some time and space to regain equilibrium. In addition to creating a supportive environment, it is helpful to offer physical comfort—*if* the individual finds that to be soothing. Options include a weighted blanket or a gentle, firm hug. Open communication during the planning sessions can help allistic people know how to respond before a meltdown occurs. In my case, I find that deep pressure is calming, so I like to have a weighted blanket or a compression vest readily available. Some autistic people respond well to sensory tools like stress balls or fidget toys, so make sure to have these items nearby.

Shutdowns are similar to meltdowns. Both are typically triggered by sensory, mental, or social overload. But a shutdown is quite different from a meltdown. During a shutdown, autistic people may become less verbal. They might be unable to communicate at all. Their movements may become slower or cease altogether. They might appear to be unresponsive to their surroundings. Their mental state is expressed with physical behaviors such as not moving, tensing the body, curling up in a fetal position, or pressing themselves into a tight space. They may also appear lethargic or even catatonic.

As with meltdowns, shutdowns can be incredibly distressing for the autistic person and for those nearby. It is essential for everyone to recognize that a shutdown is a coping mechanism for dealing with extreme stress, not a deliberate action. Shutdowns are a form of self-protection, so patience and understanding are crucial. The presence of a familiar, trusted person who offers silent support can also be comforting.

When I experience shutdowns, it feels as though I am a passenger in my own brain. My vision becomes blurry and overly sensitive to light, making it difficult to focus on anything. Other autistic individuals have reported similar sensations, such as feeling like they have retreated into a small corner of their mind or have tunnel vision. Detachment from one's surroundings can make it challenging to communicate. These experiences accentuate the importance of creating a safe and calming space during a shutdown, allowing the autistic person to gradually regain control and focus.

Understanding that shutdowns are involuntary responses to overwhelming stress is crucial for providing appropriate support. As with meltdowns, it is helpful for allistic friends, coworkers, and family members to develop a response plan in coordination with the autistic person. Here are some questions that can facilitate that conversation. What triggers your shutdowns? What strategies help you during your shutdowns? How do you recover from a shutdown? What steps are most helpful? How can family members and friends support you during a shutdown? What does not work?

Again, it is crucial to treat autistic people with respect, acceptance, kindness, and love. Responding with anger or lectures is counterproductive and can exacerbate the situation. Instead, it is best to be a quiet and calming presence. Each autistic person is unique, so it is important to consider individual sensory needs and comfort items. My comfort items include Rupert (my blanket), my weighted blanket, my tangle cushion, and my soft toys. If physical touch is comforting, offering gentle squeezes may be helpful. The key is to help the person feel supported and safe.

After a meltdown or shutdown, autistic individuals often express a variety of emotions. These feelings can include embarrassment about what others witnessed, anger at themselves for losing control, exhaustion from the emotional and physical toll, and loneliness. During these moments, it is crucial to allow the autistic person to fully experience and process these emotions. Offering reassurance that we are loved and accepted for who we are is essential for emotional recovery.

CHAPTER 5

Mental Health

Autistic people often face sensory overload, social difficulties, and stigmatization, all of which can contribute to mental health struggles. Mental health challenges are highly prevalent among autistic individuals, with research indicating that approximately 70 to 80 percent of autistic people experience mental health issues. Specifically, 66 percent of autistic people have considered suicide, 40 to 50 percent have experienced anxiety, and 40 percent have experienced depression. Those rates are far higher than what is observed among allistic populations. By comparison, about 10 to 15 percent of allistic individuals experience mental health challenges, including 14 percent who have considered suicide, 7 to 13 percent who have experienced anxiety, and 10 percent who have experienced depression. Given the much higher numbers among autistic people, it is crucial to better understand the causes of mental health issues in autistic individuals and to tailor treatment options that address our unique needs.

Effective mental health support for autistic people should accommodate sensory variations in an accepting environment. Additionally, mental health professionals should be trained to recognize and understand the specific manifestations of mental health issues in autistic individuals, which can sometimes differ from those in allistic individuals. By improving awareness and developing targeted interventions, we can better support the mental health and well-being of autistic people.

Sensory sensitivities, and intolerance to uncertainty and change, can significantly heighten anxiety in autistic people. When I was diagnosed, I was informed that much of my anxiety stemmed from sensory overload and the fear of entering overwhelming situations. Autistic individuals often rely on routines and structure, which is why uncertainties or changes can cause significant anxiety. For example, I once experienced a lot of change and uncertainty during a four-week period, which led to extremely high levels of anxiety. This, in turn, exacerbated my eating struggles. I became very sick and lost six kilos in a short span of time.

It is essential for autistic and allistic people to work together on a plan to manage triggers that cause anxiety. Because change and uncertainty are common causes of stress, everyone should think about how to maintain a regular, predictable routine. The plan should establish clear communication channels and use visual aids. When allistic people know that a change in life is on the horizon, they can give the autistic person plenty of extra time to prepare for and make the transition. In addition, professional guidance, when it is tailored to the unique needs of each autistic individual, can be very beneficial.

Here are some questions that can be used as autistic and allistic people develop a plan. In what ways do sensory overload, social interactions, or changes in routine affect your mental health? What strategies or tools do you use to effectively manage anxiety or stress? How do you cope with feelings of depression or low mood? Are there specific activities or practices that help lift your spirits? Who are the key people in your support system, and how do they help you with your mental health?

Autistic individuals with rejection sensitive dysphoria (RSD) can experience significant emotional distress in response to perceived or actual rejection. These overwhelming feelings of emotional pain can arise from any type of rejection, no matter how minor it might seem to others. For example, an interaction during which the tone or body language of the other person is off, or when the language is dismissive or critical, can be interpreted by the autistic person as a profound and personal rejection, even if the other person had no intention of causing harm. This heightened sensitivity can make ordinary social interactions particularly challenging, leading to anxiety, avoidance of social situations, and difficulties in forming and maintaining relationships. People with RSD may even *anticipate* rejection in every interaction, which again increases anxiety and causes the individual to withdraw.

Understanding and recognizing RSD can help people who support autistic individuals to communicate more effectively and empathetically, reducing the likelihood of triggering distress. For instance, Emma shared that she is very sensitive and often overthinks situations, leading to anxiety and sadness. Support strategies for individuals with RSD include using clear, reassuring, and positive communication, and being mindful of nonverbal cues. Building a supportive environment where the autistic person feels safe and valued can significantly mitigate the impact of RSD. Additionally, seeking professional support or therapy can provide autistic people with valuable coping mechanisms to manage the intense emotions associated with rejection sensitivity.

Biological factors can also increase anxiety in autistic individuals. Cortisol, a stress hormone, is released when the brain's amygdala detects a threat. Research indicates that autistic people often have an enhanced cortisol response to stress, meaning we have higher cortisol levels. Moreover, the hormone remains active in our system for a longer duration compared to allistic individuals. High levels of prolonged cortisol response results in intense anxiety during stressful situations, making it difficult to return to a baseline emotional state. Understanding these biological differences can help when developing plans and strategies for helping autistic people who struggle with anxiety.

To manage my anxiety, I use medication. Emma has tried two different medications; the first one did not work, but the second has been very effective. However, this approach may not be suitable for everyone and should be discussed with a medical professional to determine the best course of action. Other strategies can include therapy, mindfulness practices, and a strong support network. These methods can help mitigate anxiety and improve overall well-being. It is important to tailor the approach to fit each person's circumstances and preferences.

Autism awareness and acceptance can play a significant role in mitigating depression and anxiety. Autistic people should embrace autism as part of their identity and take pride in being neurodivergent. Self-acceptance is greatly influenced by the attitudes of those around the autistic person. When allistic people are knowledgeable about autism, they can show genuine curiosity and love. Acceptance by others helps autistic people pave the way for self-acceptance, which reduces feelings of isolation and improves mental well-being.

Societal acceptance and awareness—beyond close relationships—can reduce stigma, making it easier for autistic individuals to seek support and accommodations without fear of judgment. Widespread understanding and acceptance, for example in schools and workplaces, can significantly decrease anxiety and depression for autistic people. Education and open dialogue about autism contribute to a more inclusive society. This inclusivity enhances the quality of life for autistic people, and it enriches the entire community by allowing autistic people to make their unique contributions.

Mental health treatment options for autistic individuals have expanded in recent years. Traditionally, talk therapy has been widely offered, but many autistic people struggle with this approach because it is difficult for them to recognize and communicate feelings. This communication hurdle is often caused by alexithymia (the difficulty of engaging in extended conversations). New therapy options have been developed, and older approaches have been adapted specifically for autistic individuals. One example is contemplative therapy, also known as reflective integration therapy, which focuses on leveraging the individual's inherent strengths and capabilities rather than emphasizing deficits. This mode of therapy works well with my brain. I am reaping many benefits from it. Another example is cognitive-behavioral therapy (CBT). This form of therapy has been adapted to be more autism-friendly by incorporating visual aids and concrete examples. Art therapy, music therapy, and occupational therapy also provide valuable outlets for self-expression and they help build coping strategies that are aligned with the unique ways that autistic individuals experience the world.

Not all options work well for everyone. I have seen many therapists over the years and have struggled with their forms of therapy. Emma also has seen many therapists and has found it most effective when they specialize in autism. Her current therapist, who specializes in autism, has tailored her therapy room with sensory items, creating a supportive and accommodating environment. This therapist's understanding and acceptance of autistic traits have made a significant difference for Emma. She enjoys working with her therapist and finds the therapy highly beneficial because it is customized to meet her specific needs and preferences.

During my most challenging times, I often feel overwhelmed by anxiety. Anxiety is like having a tiny, hyperactive squirrel in your brain that never stops worrying about where it left its acorns. I did not find relief until I started working with a therapist who specialized in autism. Therapy helps calm the squirrel, or at least it gets the squirrel to focus on fewer acorns at a time. My therapist taught me how to use deep breathing and structured routines to regain control over my life.

Sam struggled with a therapist because it felt as if he had to educate her about his experiences rather than receiving guidance and support. Sam's experience draws attention to the need for therapists who have expertise in working with autistic individuals.

The SPACE model offers a valuable framework for creating or adapting therapeutic options to better suit the needs of autistic individuals. SPACE stands for Sensory, Predictability, Acceptance, Communication, and Empathy. This model seeks to ensure predictability in the autistic person's interactions, thereby reducing anxiety. It also fosters acceptance of the individual's unique characteristics and strengths, enhances communication strategies to suit each person's preferences, and shows empathy toward individual experiences. By incorporating these principles, therapists can provide effective and supportive care for autistic individuals, helping them feel more understood and valued in the therapeutic process.

Researchers are learning more all the time, so it is crucial for mental health professionals to stay informed about emerging approaches for helping the diverse needs of autistic individuals. Doing so will lead to better mental health care for people in the autistic community.

Beyond therapy, another effective way to help autistic people improve mental health is by enabling them to pursue special interests. Whenever I immerse myself in a special interest, I feel content, fulfilled, and invigorated. Special interests can also enhance success in schoolwork. When I was in school, I related as many assignments as possible to horses. The teachers who allowed me to make this connection saw me succeed and enjoy their classes. Conversely, those who insisted that I needed to "broaden my mind" and try other things saw me struggle and skip classes.

While engaging in a special interest, many autistic people, including myself, can enter a state of hyperfocus. This intense level of concentration allows us to focus on tasks, including schoolwork. Encouraging autistic people to pursue their special interests can significantly improve academic and social outcomes.

As I mentioned earlier in the book, autistic people often have a narrower range of special interests. Unfortunately, this leads allistic people to assume that autistic people are restricted, obsessive, or inflexible—even though these special interests are incredibly positive. They provide emotional regulation, enable us to absorb vast amounts of information, and often lead to career opportunities. Many successful individuals have embraced their autism and leveraged special interests to excel in careers. These interests foster deep knowledge and expertise, which can lead to innovative contributions in various fields.

In addition, the use of affirmations can significantly improve the mental health of autistic people. An affirmation is a positive thought or statement that suppresses negative thinking. Autistic individuals often engage in repetitive thought cycles, a key characteristic of autism. This repetition can be harnessed effectively by replacing negative thoughts with positive affirmations, which helps to silence negative self-talk and trains the brain to favor positivity.

To practice daily affirmations, start by identifying the predominant negative thoughts. Write them down, say them out loud, or just keep them in mind. Next, replace the negative thoughts with positive counterparts. It might take time, but it is possible. Instead of thinking, "I am young and naive, and no one will take me seriously," it is better to say, "Wisdom is not measured in years. I am smart, capable, and my opinion matters." I like to write my affirmations on sticky notes and place them around my house, allowing me to read them repeatedly. You can also say them out loud like a mantra, write them in a journal, record them with a phone, or use any other method that helps. Regularly engaging with these affirmations can reinforce positive thinking and boost self-esteem.

Here are some additional examples of positive affirmations that you can use to reinforce self-love and confidence: My mind is unique, and I see the world in a remarkable way; I am intelligent and valuable; I trust myself to make great decisions; I am brave and courageous; My friends appreciate me for who I am; My feelings matter; I love myself unconditionally; I am capable of overcoming challenges; I am focused and persistent; I grow stronger and more resilient every day; I choose happiness.

Through it all, autistic and allistic people can work together to improve the mental health of autistic individuals.

CHAPTER 6

Relationships

The belief that autistic people lack the desire or need for relationships, whether platonic or romantic, is false. Like all human beings, we crave and require connection with others. However, our approach to forming connections may differ from societal norms. Autistic individuals often seek meaningful connections, but our social interactions may not align with typical expectations. Those differences are perfectly acceptable.

Sam says that his most meaningful relationships are with people who are loyal, listen to his issues, offer good advice when needed, and enjoy spending time with him. For Emma, a friend is someone who cares about her, wants to spend time with her, and with whom she can be open and honest. Nate says a friend is someone who respects and cares about him and with whom he can share openly and honestly. Helen sees a friend as someone who understands and accepts her for who she is, emphasizing mutual respect and understanding in meaningful relationships.

It took a long time for me and the people in my relational circle to understand that autistic people often forge connections in unique ways. Autistic individuals may prefer deep conversations more than small talk, or they might base friendships more on shared values than on social activities. This approach is not a deficiency; it is just a different way of experiencing social bonds. Understanding and embracing these differences can lead to richer, more fulfilling relationships for everyone involved. For that matter, every person might have specific criteria for choosing friends. How do *you* define a friend? What qualities do *you* value most in a relationship?

When I was growing up, I went through life as an undiagnosed autistic girl surrounded primarily by allistic individuals who had limited knowledge about autism. I frequently received comments about being excessively "moody" or "weird." My mood swings and unconventional behaviors often became the subject of jokes and the source of disputes, even within my family. Emma experienced similar difficulties with people who misread her intentions or thought she was crazy. She also found it hard to read social cues, which made it difficult for her to understand how other people truly felt about her. Helen struggled to create and maintain friendships because people often deemed her "moody" or "uninterested" when she needed to recharge by being alone. Sam has always found it difficult to make friends. His anxiety increases when he meets someone new, which can cause him to shut down. When he encounters a new person, he often ends up not saying anything, which results in an awkward situation. When I meet someone new, I feel like I fade into the background. I sometimes forget how to speak or move, or I might shut down. These experiences highlight the importance of awareness and empathy. It is crucial for allistic people to recognize that what might seem like aloofness or moodiness is often a need for solitude and a break from sensory overload.

One strategy that can help autistic people make friendships is having a trusted person accompany the autistic individual when meeting someone new. The support person can ease the anxiety and facilitate initial interactions until the autistic person becomes more familiar with the new person. By gradually acclimating to new social settings with the help of a supportive companion, autistic individuals can navigate the complexities of forming friendships more effectively.

My difficulties with social interactions made it challenging for me to establish and maintain friendships while growing up. From primary school onward, other children would ask me why I was so weird or why I did unusual things. To fit in, I would often mask my true self (camouflaging), hiding my autistic traits to appear more "normal." This was exhausting and ultimately unsustainable, contributing to the fleeting nature of my friendships. Despite my best efforts to connect with others, these relationships typically lasted only a few days to a few months. Children can quickly judge what they do not understand, and without a framework to explain my differences, I was often left feeling isolated and misunderstood. Because I did not understand my own needs and behaviors, it was impossible to explain myself to others or to advocate for myself. Back then, I had never heard of autism.

Over time, I learned that finding genuine friendships involved being true to myself and seeking out those who accepted me as I am. Understanding and embracing my autism has been essential for forming meaningful and lasting relationships. By being authentic, I have been able to educate those around me about autism.

There is a fascinating concept known as "the uncanny valley." It refers to the eerie, unsettling feeling that creeps over you when encountering a humanoid, a robot that closely resembles a human. Something about it seems off. This is how allistic people often feel when they meet an autistic person. Research suggests that allistic individuals may have negative responses to autistic people, akin to the uncanny valley effect. In my view, allistic people have this type of reaction when the autistic person is camouflaging; that is, when an autistic individual is mimicking neurotypical behavior. Consequently, autistic individuals may exhibit what allistic people perceive as "realistic" body language, facial expressions, tone of voice, and emotions, but they still perceive that something is slightly askew. This frequently occurs during initial encounters. As research indicates, first impressions hold significant weight.

Now, autistic individuals are not robots; I can personally vouch for my humanity. We will never ask for oil changes. On websites, I always tick the "I am not a robot" box and I correctly identify all the squares with traffic lights in them. Nevertheless, allistic people often get a strange feeling because autistic people do not fit neatly with their expectations. This misalignment is exacerbated when autistic individuals try to fit into a mold that is unnatural for them. This can result in negative first impressions, which can be challenging to overcome. By recognizing that camouflaging is an autistic person's attempt to fit in, not an indication of deception or insincerity, allistic individuals can develop more empathy and patience. Awareness about autism can lead to positive and meaningful connections.

From a young age, allistic people can experience "the uncanny valley" when they interact with autistic people. Children may not understand that someone is specifically autistic, but they do recognize differences. As a result, autistic children begin to face social challenges early in life. This is why it is so important to educate allistic children at an early age about autism and other types of neurodiversity. By teaching children about neurodiversity, we can help them understand that differences in behavior, communication, and sensory experiences are natural and valuable. We can promote empathy, reduce bullying, and encourage inclusive attitudes. Simple conversations about how everyone has unique strengths and struggles can go a long way toward normalizing neurodiversity.

Schools can play a significant role in helping allistic children relate well with autistic kids by including neurodiversity in the curriculum and creating environments that accommodate various sensory and communication needs. Encouraging neurodiverse children to express their unique perspectives can build their self-esteem and resilience. And educating allistic children about neurodiversity helps them become the allies and advocates of autistic kids.

The media can also encourage deeper understandings of relationships between allistic and autistic people. *Sesame Street,* the long-running program for children, features a character (a puppet) named Julia who is autistic. Julia helps allistic children relate with autistic children who watch the show in a fun, enjoyable, and meaningful way. For adults, films like *Temple Grandin* (2010) and the TV series *Astrid* are examples of how books, movies, and other media that feature courageous neurodiverse characters, including those who are autistic, can help allistic people see neurodiversity as a normal part of life.

Overcoming Communication Barriers

It is important for allistic people to recognize that autistic people usually struggle to read and respond to social cues. For example, autistic people might find it hard to understand nonverbal communication, such as facial expressions, which can lead to misunderstandings in social situations.

Autistic people often express emotions more intensely, or they might have difficulty identifying and articulating their feelings. Partners or friends of autistic people may not understand some emotional responses. Autistic individuals might speak in monotone or have difficulty modulating their voices to convey the intended emotion, leading to misunderstandings about their feelings or intentions.

These challenges can be exhausting and stressful, but it is possible for autistic and allistic people to establish meaningful and supportive relationships with each other. It mainly takes understanding and patience. Helen emphasized that clear communication enhances her relationships. She and her friends engage in open conversations about their needs and boundaries, ensuring mutual understanding. By respecting the specific needs and preferences of the autistic person, and by working together, everyone can form resilient and supportive relationships.

Nonverbal communication is central to all relationships, but autistic people might struggle to assign meaning to nonverbal cues. I can easily detect changes in another person's facial expressions, but they often hold little meaning for me. I feel like I am trying to decipher the purpose of the bricks in the wall at the entrance to Diagon Alley in *Harry Potter*. I see the facial movements, but I cannot unlock any secret passageways that help me understand whether each change signifies happiness, frustration, boredom, or something else. Therefore, it is sometimes difficult for me to respond appropriately or maintain a fluid rhythm in conversations. I am sincerely interested in the feelings and ideas of others, but I often feel like I am trying to understand a foreign language without knowing the grammar or vocabulary.

Instead of perpetually walking on eggshells, I have learned to inquire directly about people's feelings or thoughts. Asking direct questions is a good way to avoid confusion! However, allistic people often wrongly think I am being intrusive or confrontational, which can lead them to avoid giving me an honest answer. So, I usually limit my use of this strategy to those who know me well and understand the context behind my questions. These trusted individuals offer valuable feedback and support, helping me navigate social nuances more effectively. I am thankful for the people who guide me through the labyrinth of social cues.

Another helpful approach is to learn about social interactions in a low-pressure environment. This might involve watching movies, reading books, or observing people communicate from a distance. Using written communication, such as texting or emailing, can also be advantageous. Writing allows more time to process information and craft thoughtful responses, reducing the immediate pressure of face-to-face engagements. Another strategy is to use "social stories" or role-playing to practice interpreting facial expressions and body language in a safe environment. Social stories are short narratives accompanied by pictures and words that describe an event or activity. They provide specific information about what to expect and why, making new situations more accessible and understandable. By offering clear and relatable examples, social stories can effectively demystify real-world scenarios. By combining direct inquiries with these strategies, I can more effectively engage with people, build stronger relationships, and reduce anxiety.

Beyond my struggles to interpret nonverbal cues, I sometimes have difficulty finding the hidden meanings in people's *spoken* words because there are so many nuances beneath the surface. When I miss subtle messages woven into the fabric of conversations, allistic people sometimes think I am socially naive, which is not true. The barrier

I face is only related to communication, not my understanding of the world. I sometimes take people's words at face value, which has landed me in trouble more than once.

Sarcasm and humor can be especially challenging for autistic individuals. This does not mean they are incapable of being sarcastic or humorous. I understand the concept of sarcasm and I often use it in my conversations. However, I encounter difficulty in discerning the nuanced cues within another person's sarcasm. Sarcasm often flies over my head because I struggle to quickly complete the puzzle of body language and verbal cues before responding. This challenge can be particularly evident in social interactions where sarcasm, jokes, or indirect communication are common. It can be frustrating and sometimes embarrassing when I cannot pick up on these cues.

When I was around fifteen years old, I walked into the kitchen and found that everyone in my family was peeling hard-boiled eggs. This looked like fun! I wanted to join in. I picked up an egg and inquired, "How do I crack it?"

"On your head," came the response.

Without hesitation, I enthusiastically complied. The aftermath? A faint green bruise adorning my forehead for the next few days.

This story now elicits laughter—imagine me as a cartoon character with stars circling my head—but other examples are not so humorous. Miscommunication can be painful and embarrassing. For autistic individuals, it can be difficult to decipher ulterior motives, conflicting emotions, or deceit. These subtle messages are typically conveyed through shifts in tone, body language, and facial expressions—nonverbal cues that can easily elude an autistic person's detection. The consequences of not perceiving them can be serious, including the end of relationships, the formation of unhealthy relationships, or bullying.

Allistic people—not just autistic people—create many communication problems. In fact, autistic people like me often do a better job of communication than allistic people. If the purpose of communication is mutual understanding, then the ways that allistic people typically rely on subtleties, nuances, innuendos, and "reading between the lines" is, in my view, counterproductive. It should be no surprise that allistic individuals frequently struggle with misunderstandings. I think that allistic people could benefit greatly from *my approach* to communication. I am direct and honest and clear. My words can be taken at face value. I speak candidly, saying what I mean and meaning exactly what I say.

Direct communication is ideal for autistic individuals because it streamlines social interactions. However, it is not a license to say hurtful words. The goal is to convey one's intentions, desires, needs, and thoughts clearly, ensuring mutual understanding. Communication should always be respectful and considerate, focusing on clarity rather than bluntness. It is about being honest and straightforward without causing unnecessary harm or offense.

Emma finds it challenging to discern whether someone is genuinely her friend or simply being polite. She gauges true friendship by the effort people make to communicate with her, whether through talking or messaging, and by their willingness to carve out time for her. These actions signal to her that they genuinely care about her and value her friendship. Consistent and meaningful interactions based on clear and direct communication are important for Emma when she is identifying real friends. Clarity eliminates the ambiguity that often causes stress and anxiety for autistic individuals, and it reduces misunderstandings.

Autism and Empathy

Another common misconception, which can affect relationships, is that autistic people do not feel empathy. There are two types of empathy: cognitive and affective. *Cognitive empathy* involves the ability to read facial cues, recognize and label emotions, and understand why someone feels a certain way. It requires the ability to put oneself in another person's shoes and understand that person's perspective. Research indicates that autistic individuals might have a lower capacity for engaging with people in ways that *express* cognitive empathy, at least compared to average allistic people, but this does not mean autistic people lack empathy.

Affective empathy is expressed in at least a couple of ways, such as *mirroring* another person's emotions, or *experiencing* another person's feelings. For example, if someone is feeling anxious, another person might mirror (imitate, reflect) that person's anxiety through words or nonverbal responses. In other cases, a person might sincerely *experience or feel* the anxiety of the anxious person and respond with equal distress.

Research indicates that autistic people often experience intense feelings. The people I interviewed for this book confirmed that research. Autistic people may exhibit higher levels of affective empathy than many allistic people. This does not mean all autistic individuals have high affective empathy or that they entirely lack cognitive empathy; rather, the balance between cognitive and affective empathy may differ for autistic individuals compared to allistic individuals. However, autistic people are fully capable of feeling and expressing empathy. By understanding these nuances, we can foster better communication and stronger connections.

This ties into Damian Milton's "double empathy" problem. Milton is an autistic scholar whose research posits that autistic people do not lack empathy or social skills; they simply have different ways of socializing and expressing empathy compared to allistic people. According to the double empathy theory, there is a mutual misunderstanding between autistic and allistic individuals that creates challenges in social interactions and relationships for both parties. The prevailing discourse focuses on the misunderstandings that autistic individuals have about neurotypical social norms and expressions of empathy. However, the reverse is also true. Allistic individuals frequently misunderstand how autistic people socialize and express empathy.

The double empathy problem highlights the importance of mutual understanding and adaptation. It should not be solely the responsibility of autistic individuals to adapt to allistic norms. Instead, everyone should work together to bridge the gap in understanding. This approach would improve inclusive and respectful interactions in which autistic and allistic individuals can appreciate and learn from the unique perspectives and communication styles of the other.

During my school days, I found immense pleasure in reading books day in and day out. However, I would have liked to have had a friend or two reading quietly next to me. Unfortunately, many people deem reading to be antithetical to socializing, even though this type of quiet interaction is known by researchers as "parallel play." Despite the word *play* in the phrase, parallel play is not just for children; adults also enjoy it. The idea is to share an activity alongside someone who is also occupied with an activity, perhaps

YOU, ME, AND AUTISM

without talking much. It could entail reading books in the same room, or constructing a Lego Death Star, or knitting a scarf side by side. Sam enjoys playing computer games with his friends, a time when they are together but engaged in their own activities. This form of social interaction does not necessitate constant verbal communication, which alleviates the stress and tension often associated with socializing. Parallel play is not the only mode of social engagement for autistic individuals, but it provides the comfort of companionship without the pressure of traditional social expectations, making it a valuable option for many autistic people. It allows us to seamlessly integrate our special interests with our friendships, even when we have divergent passions.

When I was growing up, I enjoyed being involved with horses. If there was an opportunity to be around horses, I seized it eagerly. Every school project, book I read, or game I played revolved around horses. If there was a way to sneak a horse into a math problem, I found it! I delved into researching horse breeds. I even compiled an alphabetical book detailing each breed's characteristics. Fortunately, my parents supported my passion, providing me with horse books, opportunities to ride, and a willingness to discuss horses for hours on end. I could talk about horses until the cows—or rather, the horses—came home.

I fondly recall a morning tea with my mother, when I was around twelve, during which I talked about horses for two hours straight, uninterrupted. Two solid hours of horse facts! Move over TED Talks! Her unwavering enthusiasm and willingness to listen brought me immense happiness and strengthened our bond. I felt truly accepted and understood. My mother's approach is a model for fostering a relationship with an autistic person, even when you do

Relationships

not share a mutual interest. By being an attentive listener, you can learn a lot. Need a fun fact about the Andalusian or the Arabian? I am your person!

Black-and-White Thinking

In recent years, I have come to realize that my tendency to think in binary, rigid, black-and-white terms might impact my friendships in ways that are deeper than I imagined. This way of thinking manifests when I insist on doing things a certain way and refuse to entertain alternative methods or perspectives. When I was a child, I had to arrange my Sylvanian toys in their rooms in a specific order. Any deviation felt inherently wrong. My style of play clashed with the desires of other children to play more freely with the toys, which led to disagreements and earned me labels like "bossy" and "boring." Similarly, during playtime with my brother and our toy cars, I insisted on organizing them according to their colors. I named each one after a rainbow color. Red cars went first, followed by orange and yellow—you get the idea. Once again, my rigidity led to me being labeled as "bossy." My brother grew disinterested in playing with me. Apparently, my color-coded car organization was not as thrilling as I thought. This left me feeling profoundly lonely and isolated. My Sylvanian toys lived in perfectly ordered bliss and my toy cars were in rainbow harmony, but I struggled alone in a not-so-black-and-white world of childhood friendships.

Rigid thinking, also known as all-or-nothing thinking, can significantly affect the social interactions and relationships of autistic individuals. The cognitive pattern is characterized by viewing situations in extremes, without recognizing nuances. It can contribute to a sense of order and predictability, but it often leads to conflicts when others do not share the same perspectives. Therefore, allistic people should approach this style of thinking with empathy and patience, helping autistic friends and family members to gradually become more flexible in their thought processes.

The tendency to think in binary, inflexible ways means that autistic people sometimes struggle to grasp the nuances and grey areas of life's complexity. For us, things are either right or wrong, healthy or unhealthy. This applies to friendships as well. We tend to perceive relationships in absolute terms, viewing someone as either a friend or not a friend, with little room for the ambiguous middle ground that often characterizes social connections. Because I find it challenging to fully comprehend the varying degrees of friendship, I often assume that everyone is a friend. If the relationship persists, I might be inclined to wrongly assume that a normal friend is a *close* friend. It can be hard for me to distinguish between someone who genuinely cares and someone who might take advantage of my openness. This mentality has made me vulnerable to manipulation, gaslighting, bullying, and exploitation. I have had to learn that acquaintances are not necessarily people with whom I should share personal details or offer unwavering loyalty.

However, with the right support, these difficulties can serve as valuable learning opportunities, and they can strengthen bonds between friends. For instance, during a dinner outing with my friend Oliver and our research supervisor, I shared something about Oliver that she did not want to disclose. I had mistakenly treated my supervisor as a friend rather than as a professional colleague. Oliver graciously understood how my brain works. This incident led to open communication between us, and it ultimately strengthened our friendship.

Black-and-white thinking can pose significant challenges as one moves from childhood into adulthood. People are usually patient with children who struggle to understand complex relational concepts. However, as an adult, everyone expects us to understand social boundaries and nuances. When autistic adults cannot meet these social expectations, they often face more barriers when trying to build genuine friendships. Autistic people feel like everyone except them has received a secret rulebook for making friendships. The pressure to understand and adhere to the unspoken rules, which autistic people often do not grasp, can be overwhelming and frustrating. Allistic people might be able to find their way through the complex maze of adult friendships with relative ease, but autistic people are just trying to find the maze's entrance without any guidance.

Despite these barriers, autistic people are fully capable of forming deep, meaningful connections. We just need more time, a good map, and perhaps a few friendly tour guides along the way. I turn to my board of trustees when I encounter a social situation that I do not understand. My support network provides valuable insights and advice, helping me navigate complex social dynamics more effectively, including romantic relationships. A board of trustees can also foster a sense of security and confidence. This network can be composed of family members, close friends, mentors, or professionals who understand the unique challenges faced by autistic individuals.

Black-and-white thinking is usually coupled with a profound aversion to change. I have always been this way. It is not a matter of disliking change per se; my struggle is with the *disruption* of consistent routines. When faced with change, my brain instinctively shuts down, adamantly refusing to accept anything new or different. My brain just says, "No, not possible." It does not matter how big or small the change is. If someone promises to wear a red shirt to dinner but shows up in a yellow one, I will struggle to adapt. My brain will go into DEFCON 1, as if the color of the shirt has upended the fabric of the universe. The unexpected shift throws everything off balance. My brain treats it like a major roadblock. And do not get me started on menu changes at my favorite restaurant. That presents a level of chaos that I am not equipped to handle!

Again, rigid thinking is rooted in an autistic person's need for predictability and control. It provides a sense of security and stability, reducing anxiety. However, black-and-white thinking can make it difficult to handle the inevitable changes and uncertainties of daily life, which can negatively affect relationships.

Despite knowing *logically* that a change may be beneficial for me, I find myself unable to accept it. For example, I love drinking strawberry milk and have always used a particular brand of powder. One time, my parents bought a different brand of strawberry powder. The new brand tasted better, but my brain said, "No, I don't like it." Try explaining that logic—"It tastes better, but I am not drinking it"—to your parents. It is incredibly frustrating for me, but my brain refuses to cooperate with changes. Any deviation from the norm, even if it is an improvement, can trigger anxiety and discomfort. The brain's automatic response is to seek stability above all else.

To help autistic people cope with aversion to change, allistic people can gradually introduce new plans. Instead of making a sudden switch, they can introduce small variations incrementally. Start by mixing a little of the new with the old. This can help ease the transition and allow the autistic person to adjust more comfortably.

Another helpful approach is to create a structured plan. Autistic individuals like to know what to expect and to have a step-by-step guide. It will help autistic people if they understand why the change is occurring. It is also important to recognize the signs of an impending shutdown or meltdown and then take proactive mitigation steps, as I described earlier. Working with the autistic person, an allistic friend or relative can write down the benefits and positive aspects of the change, which can reinforce logical thinking and gradually overcome initial resistance. Even if a new plan causes me to have had a meltdown, I can usually accept the change if given sufficient time to analyze and understand it logically. In these situations, patience and understanding from those around me are invaluable.

It also helps autistic people to embrace change when allistic friends and family members offer the autistic person a range of choices within the parameters of the situation. In addition, allistic people can emphasize that other aspects of the situation will not change, such as the permanence of friendships, familial support, or special interests.

As with other aspects of autism, black-and-white thinking is not a weakness. It should be seen as a remarkable strength, one that allistic people often lack. My preference for routines and structure correlate with my organizational skills and meticulous attention to detail. I possess the ability to thoroughly research and plan any endeavor, demonstrating an extraordinary capacity to remember details, such as a person's favorite baked good and how to prepare it. By planning, organizing, and remembering such details, I am empowered to establish structure in my daily life and accomplish a lot with great efficiency. Organizational skills help me to maintain a predictable routine, and they allow me to excel in tasks that require precision and thoroughness.

My attention to detail also enables me to create personalized experiences for others, enhancing my relationships. Remembering someone's favorite treat or preferred activities shows that I care about them. I mean, who would not love a batch of their favorite cookies or a movie night featuring their all-time favorite film? When I am attentive to the preferences of others, I can shift my focus from the unpredictable aspects of relationships to engaging in well-prepared, thoughtful activities. My friends always know they can count on me for the most meticulously planned and enjoyable gatherings. Who needs spontaneity when you have precision and cookies?

However, my reliance on routines and structure often exceeds the habits of other people. To avoid surprises, I thoroughly prepare before going anywhere. For example, if I am going to a seminar or conference, I check who will be there, prepare scripts for potential conversations, and consult a digital map (even if I am not driving) to familiarize myself with the location and its appearance. I decide what to wear, choose my seating if possible, or enlist someone to help me decide where to sit when we arrive. I ask a colleague to walk me to the bathroom when needed. (My bathroom buddy system is legendary.) I prepare for specific activities and study food options ahead of time. This level of preparation is necessary for me to feel secure and comfortable in social settings. By the time the event arrives, I often find myself mentally drained!

Relationships

Avoiding Burnout

As you might expect, autistic people face extensive barriers when seeking to form and maintain strong relationships. Mental, emotional, and physical exhaustion can impact the quality of relationships between autistic and allistic people. The mental energy required for me to make detailed plans, for example, can leave me feeling exhausted. Support from understanding friends and family who can help is invaluable. Autistic people sometimes refrain from seeking help because they have been teased, or because they do not want to be a burden. So, allistic people should take the initiative and offer assistance with kindness and understanding. When autistic individuals feel supported and understood in their need for preparation, it enhances trust and communication.

Beyond receiving support from others, autistic people can apply some helpful tools to manage energy levels. One involves the use of spoons. You probably think I am referring to those little utensils for eating, but I am referring to spoons in a metaphorical sense. It is called the "spoons theory." Picture your brain as the kitchen drawer where you keep spoons. Each time you use a spoon you expend some mental energy. You wake up in the morning with fifty spoons. You use three spoons to shower, another two to get dressed, and five to make and eat breakfast. Then you use one spoon to pack your bag and four to drive to your friend's house. Throughout the day, you spend ten spoons to be with your friend. By the time the evening rolls around, you have just enough spoons left to drive home and prepare dinner. Cooking dinner with your last few spoons can feel like you are participating in an extreme sport. If you run out

YOU, ME, AND AUTISM

of spoons before you make dinner, it will be game over until you can restock the spoons. That is your day, carefully measured out in spoons.

Now, imagine if you start the day with only twenty spoons instead of fifty. The same tasks suddenly become more challenging to manage. Showering, dressing, and eating breakfast already consume a significant portion of your limited energy, leaving you with fewer spoons for the rest of the day. This is a common experience for autistic individuals. They need to carefully manage energy to avoid a burnout. Certain activities may require more energy on some days than they do on others. On days when my spoon count is low, my capacity to engage in social situations diminishes, which means I may appear distant or unresponsive. And that can affect relations with friends and family members.

This is when the relationships between autistic and allistic people become so important. When my energy levels are low, it helps to have support from friends or family members. For instance, my dad helped me write a conversation script before I made a phone call to a mechanic about my car. He told me what the shop owners would most likely ask during the call. We prepared my answers and then we made a practice phone call. When my spoon count is low, this type of support boosts my confidence and helps me navigate social interactions more smoothly.

I unabashedly ask for help. My friends and family do not force me to do anything; they simply try to help me feel more comfortable with new situations or when I lack energy. They provide support with kindness and understanding, which alleviates anxiety. However, each autistic person has unique preferences and needs, so what works for one individual may not work for another. The key is to communicate openly and find strategies that provide the necessary support without causing additional stress or discomfort.

Relationships and Expressing Emotions

Deeply affecting relationships between autistic and allistic people is the difficulty that many autistic individuals encounter when interpreting and expressing their emotions. As previously mentioned, this is known as *alexithymia*. Alexithymia is characterized by an inability to identify and describe one's own emotions. For autistic individuals, it can be challenging to process feelings and communicate them to others effectively. This difficulty in emotional expression can lead to misunderstandings because others may misinterpret the autistic person's silence or apparent lack of emotion as indifference.

Autistic people often feel intense emotions, but they might struggle to articulate them, which can lead to frustration and a sense of being misunderstood—another setback for forming deep, meaningful relationships. Therefore, creating a supportive environment where they feel safe to explore and express their emotions is essential. This might involve using alternative communication methods, such as writing or art.

Moreover, it is important to educate the autistic person's friends and family about alexithymia. Education can produce peace of mind and patience. Encouraging open, nonjudgmental communication can help autistic individuals to feel more comfortable sharing their emotions, even if it takes time. Professional support, such as therapy, can also be beneficial. Therapists can work with autistic individuals to develop strategies for identifying and expressing emotions. They can also help educate loved ones about how to better support and understand their emotional experiences.

Being able to communicate about one's emotions plays an important role in romantic relationships. These relationships can involve partnerships between two autistic individuals or between autistic and allistic individuals. In romantic relationships, meaningful and emotional conversations are pivotal while growing closer, resolving conflicts, and making long-term plans. For these reasons, it is crucial for allistic people to understand the difficulties that autistic people have when expressing their emotions. Adjusting to these dynamics can be frustrating and challenging for both partners. There is typically a period of adaptation as each partner learns to understand the other's emotional language.

When both partners are autistic, they might have a deep understanding of their common challenges and experiences, which can foster a strong connection. However, it can still be challenging for an autistic couple to navigate each other's specific communication styles and sensory needs. By comparison, when one partner is autistic and the other is allistic, the allistic partner will need to learn about autism and the unique ways in which the partner might perceive and communicate emotions. Patience, empathy, and a willingness to adapt are crucial.

Based on my personal experiences and research, I have discovered strategies that can be helpful in these situations. As stated earlier, it can be frustrating for autistic people to identify and articulate emotions with words. So, one solution is to temporarily set aside the task of labeling emotions and instead use a scale of one to ten. For example, at a social function, someone might notice changes in my body language or facial expression and ask how I am feeling on a scale of one to ten—one being the worst and ten being the best. This way, I do not have to use a word to describe a specific emotion. I can simply say I feel like a three or a four. If I am unsure, I can say something like, "I might be a three or a seven." The scale can work like an emotional weather forecast—partly cloudy with a chance of rainbows!

This numerical approach provides a straightforward method for conveying emotional states without the pressure of pinpointing exact feelings. It can be especially useful in high-stress environments where emotions are complex and difficult to untangle. Additionally, it opens a line of communication that is more accessible, allowing both partners to better understand each other. Incorporating this method into regular check-ins with each other can also strengthen relationships.

Moreover, using this scale can help track emotional patterns over time. Partners can recognize triggers or situations that consistently lead to lower or higher numbers, enabling them to make adjustments that improve overall well-being. For instance, if social events frequently result in lower numbers, the couple can develop strategies to make these events more manageable, such as taking breaks or creating a quiet space for downtime.

Autistic people can also use the numerical scale method to describe how they are feeling physically, without feeling constrained by words. Or they can use descriptors inspired by nature, colors, temperature, or drawings. For instance, an autistic person might describe feelings with descriptors such as a calm ocean, a stormy sky, or warm sunlight. Using colors to represent feelings can be another effective strategy. Expressing emotions with words like blue and calm or red and tense can convey complex emotions succinctly. It is like painting a picture of a person's mood. No art degree required!

These communication methods—visual descriptors and the numerical scale—can also promote self-awareness. By regularly tuning into the body's sensations and finding creative ways to express those sensations, autistic people can better understand their own emotional landscape. This can be helpful during times of stress or confusion when pinpointing specific emotions feels impossible. These methods provide alternative routes to emotional clarity, allowing for more accurate self-expression.

The autistic person's board of trustees can offer invaluable support by listening carefully, noting how the numbers on the scale correlate with various experiences, and deciphering which colors represent various underlying emotions. For example, everyone might see that feeling "green" corresponds to a sense of calmness. The board of trustees can also track patterns over time, making it easier to recognize recurring themes within emotional experiences. They can assist the autistic person in identifying how various situations trigger emotional states. Furthermore, the board of trustees can alleviate the autistic person's burden of navigating emotions alone. They can offer validation and reassurance. Their external perspective can provide the autistic person with a better self-understanding.

Overcoming Loneliness

At the beginning of this chapter, I stated that autistic individuals desire and benefit from relationships. They also make immense contributions to other people, offering valuable qualities such as direct communication, authenticity, loyalty, organizational skills, attention to detail, and innovative ways of expressing emotions. These unique traits can enrich relationships and foster deeper connections.

However, autistic individuals also face significant challenges when trying to build healthy relationships. Like many other autistic people, I spent much of my life grappling with feelings of isolation and profound loneliness, which was difficult to put into words and often felt insurmountable.

Understanding these dynamics is crucial for fostering supportive and meaningful relationships with autistic individuals. By recognizing the unique strengths and challenges that autistic people bring to their relationships, we can create more inclusive and empathetic environments. This involves not only appreciating their contributions but also being mindful of the difficulties we face.

I count myself fortunate to now have several close friends whose presence fills my life with immense happiness. My fervent wish is that no one experiences loneliness again.

CHAPTER 7

Education and Employment

In this chapter, I write about education and employment because many strategies are applicable in both settings. The approaches discussed here can be implemented across primary, secondary, and tertiary education settings, and in professional workplaces. The core principles of providing support, fostering understanding, and promoting inclusivity remain consistent, whether in an educational or professional environment.

In both settings, there are many problems to solve. A significant number of autistic individuals have experienced bullying during their school years. In primary school, I loved to read because it was fun and because I was severely bullied by other students who chased me, hid from me, called me names, and threw things at me. As a result, the school library became my refuge during breaks, providing a safe space away from the bullying. The library gave me an opportunity to immerse myself in the comfort of books.

Then my school decided to split lunchtime and rotate those who could be in the library, so I could only spend half the time there. The rest of the time, I had to find other ways to avoid bullies. Sometimes a teacher would require me to join a group of students outside, which was not appealing. The school's intention to encourage outdoor activities was understandable; however, forcing me into certain activities without considering my individual circumstances was not helpful. Moreover, the school did not educate my peers about autism or create supportive environments for students like me. My experience illustrates why educators need to better support neurodivergent students. Schools can do more to create safer spaces for all students to thrive.

Autistic individuals face numerous challenges in the classroom, including social interactions, sensory difficulties, and issues with instructions and structure. There are many solutions to these challenges, but autistic people and their family members might be unaware of the accommodations they can request. Group work, for instance, can be challenging for autistic people because it requires constant social interaction. During group projects, I often did not know when to speak, so I remained silent and could not fully contribute. Group work can be problematic when allistic students fail to complete their portion of the work, or when the group decides to change the project's tasks. As I described earlier, changes in an autistic person's life can cause emotional dysregulation and lead to a meltdown or shutdown.

Parents and students can ask the teacher to allow the autistic person to work individually rather than in a group. Another option is to permit the autistic student to choose group members with whom the student feels most comfortable. This accommodation benefits the autistic student and provides an opportunity for students and teachers to learn about different types of people and how to create an inclusive environment for them. Additionally, schools can implement structured group work strategies, such as assigning specific roles within the group or providing clear, step-by-step instructions to help autistic students navigate social interactions more effectively.

When autistic people exhibit dysregulated behaviors in front of others, it can further alienate them from their peers, increasing stress and anxiety. By the time I reached high school, my anxiety was at an all-time high, causing me to faint and become physically ill from stress, which significantly affected my education. Three strategies helped me in these situations.

First, schools can provide a pass that allows the autistic student to leave the classroom as needed to find a safe space for self-regulation. A pass gives autistic students the autonomy to manage sensory and emotional needs without drawing undue attention to themselves.

Second, teachers can allow autistic students to choose a seat. In most cases, autistic people prefer to be near the door, which can help minimize the stress of seating changes and make it easier to leave discreetly when needed. This simple adjustment can significantly reduce anxiety and improve the student's overall classroom experience.

Third, schools can offer autistic students the option of completing some or all education through correspondence or online, which can provide a more flexible and less stressful learning environment. This approach is common at the tertiary level, but it is not often used in primary and secondary schools. Implementing this option can help students manage their workloads and stress levels more effectively.

Schools should also foster supportive classroom environments by educating allistic students about autism. When students better understand the nature of autism, they are less likely to treat autistic peers poorly. Incorporating social-emotional learning (SEL) programs can equip students with the skills to manage emotions and build positive relationships, further bridging the gap between autistic students and their peers.

Sensory Experiences in Schools and Workplaces

Sensory difficulties can profoundly impact an autistic individual's daily life. (See chapter 3 for more on this topic). Classrooms or office environments often present sensory challenges, such as bright lights, visual clutter, noise, and crowded spaces where people often bump into each other. These sensory experiences can overwhelm autistic individuals, hindering their ability to effectively learn or work. Sam found that noisy classrooms constantly distracted and overwhelmed him. During these times, his teacher's aides were often preoccupied with other children, which left him with less support precisely when he needed it most.

Some autistic individuals, those who are hypersensitive, require reduced sensory stimulation to optimize learning and productivity. However, this does not mean that schools and companies need to strip away all sensory elements to establish autism-friendly classrooms or workspaces. Instead, companies can reduce the number of colorful posters and signs on walls, dim the lights, or designate sensory-friendly areas for autistic individuals to work. Such spaces might permit the use of noise-cancelling headphones, provide access to a secluded area or quiet corner, or allow autistic individuals to wear sunglasses indoors.

During my school years, I often preferred sitting in the back corner of the classroom, which helped me manage the noise and avoid being bumped into. Teachers frequently misunderstood this

Education and Employment

preference, thinking that I was not paying attention. Sometimes they would insist that I sit at the front of the class, which increased sensory input and made it impossible for me to concentrate on the lesson. As a result, I could not absorb the content, often missed instructions, and got into trouble. It was hard to focus on math when I felt like I was in the middle of a sensory circus. My heightened anxiety from sensory overload made me physically ill, causing me to miss school or skip class. Other autistic students have different needs, so it is important to learn about and accommodate the specific preferences of each person.

Some autistic people, those who are hyposensitive, need to move about and seek sensory stimulation. This need is often at odds with a common classroom requirement for students to sit still in their seats. This can be challenging for autistic individuals who learn and work best when they can move and fidget. Allowing them to move, however, can create a dilemma: If the teacher allows the autistic student to move about, it can distract other students. One way to solve this tension is for teachers to incorporate movement breaks into the class routine throughout the day. This method allows autistic students to move around with the other children, which also fosters a sense of belonging. However, because some autistic students may not want to move, it is best not to force group activities on them. In workplace settings, it can help autistic workers to have opportunities for regular movement breaks, such as short walks.

Other helpful strategies include allowing students and workers to choose how and where to sit. For example, some autistic people prefer to sit on their feet. Schools and workplaces can also provide flexible seating options, such as standing desks or exercise balls. By creating accommodating environments, teachers can help all

YOU, ME, AND AUTISM

students succeed and feel comfortable, and employers can improve worker productivity.

The Challenge of Processing Instructions

Processing and following instructions can be complicated for autistic individuals, depending on how the instructions are communicated. When instructions are given verbally all at once, autistic individuals often struggle to process and remember them. When presented with a series of instructions, I typically retain only the last one. This tendency sometimes leads to amusing situations. For example, if I am driving and instructed to "turn left, proceed straight after the roundabout, and then turn right," I might immediately turn right into a random driveway. Surprise! I have arrived at a stranger's house uninvited.

However, the challenge of processing instructions becomes less amusing and more distressing in a classroom or office setting with numerous peers. For instance, if a teacher instructs the class to run around the field once and then retrieve our bags and books, I might immediately collect the books, resulting in a public reprimand. "Why aren't you following instructions?" Autistic people do not intentionally disregard instructions; rather, we struggle to retain all of them.

To help mitigate this difficulty, teachers or supervisors can write the instructions on a whiteboard or on a piece of paper. They can divide the instructions into clear, manageable steps. This approach provides a visual reference that can be revisited as needed, reducing the pressure to remember everything at once.

Education and Employment

Visual supports are invaluable tools that should be customized to align the specific needs of the autistic individual with the instructional subject matter or workplace tasks. Images, written words, and other visual aids can enable autistic people to tackle tasks one step at a time. I rely heavily on written lists to keep track of my work. These strategies, supported by research and the lived experiences of autistic people, are proven to enhance learning and work opportunities.

Customizing visual supports to suit individual needs is essential. Some autistic people may prefer color-coded charts whereas others might prefer simple black-and-white lists. These tools help organize thoughts and tasks, providing a clear structure that can reduce anxiety and increase productivity. Furthermore, visual supports can be used to set clear expectations and timelines, aiding in time management and ensuring that tasks are completed efficiently.

In classroom settings, autistic students often struggle to retain verbal information during lectures, which can undermine their ability to take exams. They may miss important notes and key information. One helpful accommodation, often provided by universities, is the use of a notetaker during lectures. This type of personal help ensures that students have access to comprehensive and accurate notes without the pressure of keeping up with the pace of the lecture.

It might take autistic individuals longer to understand and respond to exam questions. Emma said that it would have helped her if she had been given extra time to complete tests. Autistic people also benefit from distraction-free test environments. By creating an equitable learning environment, educators can reduce anxiety and enable autistic students to demonstrate their true capabilities, leading to a more accurate assessment of their knowledge and skills. Similarly, employers can provide autistic workers with distraction-free environments and, when needed, allow them additional time to complete the work.

To help autistic workers and students better process instructions and information, it is helpful to maintain a consistent routine for them. It can be daunting to face activities without any preparation. At school, a teacher can write the daily schedule on a whiteboard each morning and consistently allocate specific time blocks for each subject. At work, supervisors can assist autistic employees by creating a work timetable. By reducing unknowns and designing a steady routine, employers can help autistic people to shift their focus away from worrying about uncertainties so that they can concentrate on work assignments. Research indicates that implementing such techniques can significantly improve autistic students' academic performance and classroom participation. These techniques will also improve the productivity of autistic workers within their companies.

The Rights of Autistic People

Laws in most countries require schools and companies to provide accommodations designed to support autistic students and workers. For example, in New Zealand, under the Ministry of Social Development, employers must not discriminate against a person because of a disability, and they are obligated to provide reasonable accommodations for their employees' disabilities. Reasonable accommodations are defined as "necessary and appropriate modifications and adjustments not imposing a disproportionate burden, where needed in a particular case, to ensure persons with disabilities the enjoyment or exercise on an equal basis with others of all human rights and fundamental freedoms." These accommodations apply to job advertisements, application processes, interviews, recruitment procedures, training, promotions, and job protection. Reasonable accommodations include, but are not limited to, flexible work hours, working from home, job sharing, and providing ergonomic workstations. When it comes to education and employment, it is crucial to be aware of your rights in the country or state where you reside.

Despite these provisions, it can be difficult to navigate the process of requesting reasonable accommodations. Emma found that her employers were unwilling to provide the support she requested, which is a common experience among autistic individuals. Emma wishes her employers had been more willing to adapt to her needs. She hoped to be treated with kindness rather than criticism and negativity. Nate told me that his employers took advantage of his kind nature by asking him to perform extra tasks beyond his role, without compensation. His managers justified this by saying he should be grateful for the opportunities. Nate's work challenges were exacerbated by managers who did not understand his unique strengths and challenges, a common experience for many autistic individuals. If employers were more patient and knowledgeable about neurodiversity and different learning styles, the work environment would greatly improve. Employers could benefit from the strengths of autistic people while fostering a stronger, more diverse team and better morale.

YOU, ME, AND AUTISM

When seeking accommodations, autistic people should involve a support person, such as a parent, friend, or board of trustees member. This person can provide moral support, help with communication, and reduce stress. The support person can add clarity during important meetings while ensuring that all relevant points are covered during the conversation. Autistic individuals can also use email to request accommodations from teachers or supervisors. Writing an email message reduces anxiety, allows the autistic person to clearly outline the request, and provides a written record.

Two members of my board of trustees, Oliver and Grace, assisted me in communicating my needs and requesting accommodations from my employer. We discussed the challenges I faced at work and brainstormed potential solutions. Oliver and Grace then drafted the email while I articulated my needs aloud. Together we crafted an email that clearly conveyed my needs and ensured there were no misunderstandings. Consequently, my employer acknowledged my strengths, recognized me as an asset to the team, and agreed to the requested accommodations. This made my work environment much more welcoming and allowed me to complete my tasks with high quality. The accommodations I requested included working primarily from home, being treated as an equal and not being infantilized, and being able to wear earplugs when needed. I am grateful to have such an understanding employer. This experience demonstrated the importance of having a support group who can advocate for the autistic person.

That said, it is important to think carefully about who should be on the support team. Sam had a teacher's aide for part of his schooling, but usually Sam was not provided with enough support;

therefore, his twin brother, Jack, was asked to step in to support Sam instead. This placed significant pressure on Jack, especially in relation to developing his own identity apart from Sam. Jack frequently described his experience by using the term *parentified* because he effectively became a third parent to Sam. Teachers would often ask him to support Sam, which made Jack feel overwhelmed. Demands to focus his attention on Sam left little time for Jack's own schooling and friendships. Jack felt a strong duty to support his brother, but this led to increased anxiety over the years. Sam's parents were concerned that this dynamic might affect the siblings' relationship, but fortunately it did not weaken their bond. Jack remains firm in the belief that Sam should be treated with the same respect as anyone else. Nevertheless, Jack's increased anxiety made it hard for him to attend school and interact with others. He mentioned that it would have been nice if people had asked if he was okay, too. This affirms the importance of addressing the emotional needs of siblings, who often feel overlooked.

Jack's story illustrates why, at least in most cases, it should not be the responsibility of a sibling to care for an autistic brother or sister. Siblings of autistic individuals have the same rights to friendships, sports, education, and normal sibling dynamics as any other person. They deserve the opportunity to explore their identities without being burdened by caregiving and parenting responsibilities. This is why comprehensive support services are so important. They can significantly benefit autistic individuals *and their families.* The best support services might include counseling for siblings, respite care for parents, and educational resources to help siblings and parents understand autism.

Accessing support services can be challenging, sometimes

because of reduced government funding. Therefore, it is crucial to make requests for support, which is usually a legal right, in the most effective ways possible. When making requests for accommodations at school or work, autistic people and their support groups should communicate with positive language that demonstrates how these improvements will also help the employer or teachers. For example, an autistic person could say, "I write very well when I do not have to manage sensory overload. Can I please wear my noise-canceling headphones in the classroom so that I can do my best work?" In work settings, the autistic person might say something like this: "I have a strong capacity for high productivity when I have a set routine. Would it be possible to discuss an adjustment to my daily work schedule so that I can make a better contribution to the company?"

While I pursued a PhD, my university granted my requests for accommodations to support my academic endeavors. These accommodations included studying predominantly from home to mitigate sensory overload, receiving advance notice of changes along with explanations for their occurrence, and having clear communication regarding the priority and deadlines of tasks. Like many other autistic individuals, I struggle to prioritize tasks and often attempt to tackle everything simultaneously, which can lead to burnout. Knowing this about me, my professors and supervisors provided accommodations to help me, which in turn enabled me to do better research. All that reflected well on the university!

The Challenge of Finding Employment

Many autistic individuals struggle to secure full-time employment, or any employment at all. Sometimes employers do not want to provide accommodations for autistic people. Many people in human resources departments do not understand autism, which can lead some employers to evaluate autistic candidates based on negative stereotypes. Problems can also emerge in cases when an autistic person is offered a job. The employer, perhaps after a positive interview, may erroneously conclude that the autistic worker does not require support. The hiring manager might conclude that the autistic person is not "autistic enough" to receive support.

These misperceptions underscore the importance of educating employers and coworkers about the diverse presentations of autism. It is important to help business leaders foster inclusive and accommodating work environments. Autistic people are not cookie-cutter copies. We are more like a variety pack, each with our own unique flavor.

For many autistic individuals, the interview process can be a significant barrier to employment. Helen found job interviews to be stressful due to the social expectations and the pressure to mask. Traditional interviews often emphasize social skills and the ability to think on one's feet, which can be challenging for autistic people. Employers can improve this process by offering alternative methods of assessment. For instance, they can provide interview questions and an outline of the interview format in advance thereby allowing autistic candidates time to prepare thoughtful responses. Allowing written responses as an alternative to verbal interviews can also be beneficial. Creating a more structured and predictable interview environment can alleviate anxiety, making it easier for autistic candidates to showcase their skills and qualifications.

It is crucial for workplaces to actively support autistic employees. I have already discussed the importance of various physical and sensory accommodations. In addition, peer support and mentorship programs can be highly effective ways of helping autistic individuals be productive. A mentor who offers guidance and support can significantly enhance the work experience and overall job satisfaction of autistic workers. Employers should also encourage a culture in which autistic employees feel comfortable disclosing their needs without fear of stigma or discrimination. Autism is expressed uniquely in each person, which means that the nature and extent of support may vary. A person who appears to manage well in certain situations may face significant challenges in others. Support should be based on individual needs rather than superficial judgments about "levels of autism." This inclusive approach ensures that all autistic individuals can lead fulfilling lives with access to the resources and accommodations they need.

Finally, the provision of accommodations at work or in schools does not confer an advantage to autistic people; rather, the accommodations give freedom to autistic people to fully express their talents, knowledge, passions, and intelligence. By leveling the playing field, autistic people can make a full contribution to the world and live a rewarding life.

CHAPTER 8

Disclosure

Disclosing an autism diagnosis is a personal decision that can be quite complex, depending on the situation. The experience can vary significantly for those diagnosed earlier in life compared to those diagnosed later. Individuals with an early diagnosis often rely on parents to share the information because they might be too young to understand or explain autism. Early diagnosis can shape their early experiences and interactions, sometimes leading to immediate support and understanding from those around them. By contrast, those diagnosed later in life may face other challenges. Friends and relatives might be skeptical about the truth of the diagnosis, or they might struggle to accept autism as an element of the person's identity. This can be particularly difficult if the autistic person's behavior and coping mechanisms have already been misinterpreted for years.

Regardless of when the diagnosis occurs, autistic individuals usually struggle to decide when and with whom to share the information. They experience a tension between fostering stronger relationships, by being transparent, and mitigating the risk of judgment and discrimination, by withholding information. Making this decision involves weighing the potential benefits of receiving accommodations against the risk of stigma and misunderstanding.

The stigma surrounding autism can be a daunting factor when deciding whether to disclose a diagnosis. Autism is often referred to as an "invisible" condition because there are no physical characteristics that define it. Stigma is rooted in a lack of comprehensive understanding about autism. Nevertheless, it is a reality that can influence whether an autistic adult or the parents of an autistic child choose to disclose an autism diagnosis. In an educational setting, parents may be uncertain whether sharing the diagnosis will increase their child's risk of being bullied and excluded, or whether disclosure will open doors to support, understanding, and accommodations from students and teachers. Parents may also worry that an autism diagnosis, when placed on their child's official school record, will negatively impact their child's chances of success.

In a work environment, the disclosure of autism also involves risks. Autistic workers cannot be certain whether they will face prejudice and discrimination or be met with accommodation and acceptance. The fear of being misunderstood, judged, or treated unfairly can be intense, requiring a careful assessment of the potential benefits and drawbacks in each unique situation.

When disclosing an autism diagnosis, many autistic individuals worry that friends and coworkers will think they suddenly have a different identity, as if autism has completely redefined them. That is never the case. A person might be autistic, but that fact does not fundamentally change the person's entire identity. For many, the diagnosis simply explains why an autistic person experiences and responds to life differently.

Emma told me that disclosing her autism felt like a major "coming out" experience. She believes that disclosure of autism should not be such a big deal. She wishes that her disclosure could have been straightforward—just an acknowledgment of who she is. It is about saying, "This is me, and this is who I am." Sharing about being autistic, she said, should not cause others to perceive her in a new way. For her, the goal of disclosure is to foster understanding and acceptance in light of the revealed information.

Some autistic people fear that disclosing their autism will be used as an excuse to treat them poorly. For example, they might hesitate to inform doctors or hospitals about their diagnosis because medical professionals might be uninformed about autism, which could lead them to dismiss medical conditions as being related to autism. Similarly, some autistic individuals are concerned about revealing their autism to emergency services, fearing they will not be taken seriously. These fears emerge because autistic people are very aware of the widespread ignorance about autism in society. They know that wrong perceptions about autism can lead to discrimination and neglect. Thus, the decision whether to disclose or occlude one's autism is an anxiety-inducing process.

Autistic people fear a range of damaging behaviors, including bullying, discrimination, prejudice, and infantilization. The first three are widely recognized, but infantilization is less frequently discussed. Infantilization occurs when someone is treated like a child, as if they are incapable of handling their own affairs. It can be experienced as a form of microaggression. Many autistic adults encounter infantilization after disclosing their diagnosis, which is incredibly frustrating and condescending. This type of microaggression often hides behind the guise of help, because the allistic person assumes that the autistic individual is incapable of doing anything without help. Autistic people do face challenges, but when allistic people observe a struggle in one area of an autistic person's life, they often wrongly assume that the person is not capable of doing anything. This kind of illogical assumption and behavior can severely undermine an autistic person's sense of self-worth, confidence, and autonomy.

The infantilization of autistic people might also originate from the misconception that autism is a childhood condition that people can outgrow, which is false. Autism is a developmental condition present from birth. The presentation of autism may change slightly over a person's lifespan, but it is not something that can be outgrown.

Infantilization can also lead to a self-fulfilling prophecy. If an independent autistic person is consistently treated as if they are incapable, they might start to believe it and act accordingly, which can severely undermine the person's confidence and autonomy. Autistic adults should be treated with the same respect and consideration as any other adult. It is crucial to remember that autistic individuals, regardless of age, have unique strengths and capabilities, often surpassing those of allistic people.

When autistic individuals disclose their condition, they might receive invalidating responses such as, "You don't look autistic," or, "You can't be autistic because of x, y, and z." Sam has noticed that people sometimes appear shocked when he tells them he is autistic because he does not fit the stereotypical image. Helen has experienced dismissive and judgmental reactions when she tells people about her autism. Allistic people might say things like, "You don't act like you are autistic." What exactly do they expect autistic people to act like? Do they think we walk around reciting train schedules, as if we are all Sheldon Cooper?

To avoid these types of interactions, or worse, many autistic individuals who were diagnosed later in life have developed strong camouflaging skills. As a result, allistic people might disregard the disclosure of an autistic person. This dismissal can damage the relationship between autistic and allistic people. It perpetuates the

Disclosure

stigma surrounding autism, making it more challenging for autistic individuals to seek the support and acceptance they need.

The Tensions Parents Face

Parents face a difficult decision about when to disclose an autism diagnosis to their child. Many studies suggest that telling children earlier is beneficial. Doing so allows the children to learn sooner about their brain and to understand the unique ways they experience the world. Parents can also foster a positive autistic identity early in the child's life. Research indicates that autistic children who were informed about their diagnosis later in life often felt disappointed, believing it would have been easier to grow up with that knowledge rather than receiving the information as a shock later in life.

Helen was diagnosed at age four. Her parents began explaining her autism diagnosis to her at about age five. At that time, Helen and her peers were starting to notice and question some differences between her and others. As Helen began to develop a greater awareness of her surroundings and interactions, her parents thought it would be best to start the conversation. They started with simple language, avoided medical terms, and focused on concepts she could understand. They framed the conversation positively, emphasizing that everyone's brain worked differently. Her parents explained that Helen had a unique way of seeing and experiencing the world.

As Helen moved into her early teens, when she could understand complex concepts, her parents provided more detailed explanations about autism. They always encouraged her to ask questions and talk with them about autism, continuously assuring her they would support her. Helen said this created a safe environment for her to express her thoughts and feelings. Gradually, her parents involved her in decisions related to her autism, such as choosing therapies and discussing school accommodations. This type of affirmation made her feel more in control and understood. In fact, she wishes she could have been involved in those decisions even before her early teens.

Helen's story underscores the importance of age-appropriate communication and ongoing dialogue about autism. It also highlights the value of involving autistic individuals in decisions about their care and accommodations from an early age. Doing so fosters a sense of agency and understanding. Early disclosure can also help children develop self-awareness and self-advocacy skills, which are essential in social and educational environments. By understanding their own needs and differences from a young age, autistic children can better communicate with teachers, peers, and (eventually) employers. Furthermore, early awareness can help to prevent feelings of isolation and confusion, because autistic children will understand that their experiences are a common and natural part of being human.

Autistic individuals frequently say that their parents' perceptions of and communication about autism significantly shaped their own perceptions. Unfortunately, when parents lead young children through the diagnostic process, they often encounter negative language that focuses heavily on deficits. This process is often lengthy, distressing, and overwhelming for parents, which impacts their perspective about autism. Without support, they can pass along this negative tone to their children, which may contribute to the child's feelings of inadequacy or low self-esteem. By contrast, if parents focus on the child's strengths and frame the diagnosis positively, the child will be more likely to develop a healthy, self-confident identity.

Parents face the triple challenge of processing their child's diagnosis, communicating with their child about the diagnosis, and sharing with others to advocate for support. These challenges can have a profound emotional impact on parents. Additionally, parents must find ways to care for themselves as they advocate for their child's needs in educational and social settings. All this underscores the importance of support networks and resources for parents. Connecting with other parents of autistic children, seeking guidance from autism professionals, and accessing reliable information can help parents manage these challenges more effectively.

The Journey to Self-Acceptance

The negative perceptions that some parents have about autism often become evident when they disclose their child's diagnosis. Consequently, the child internalizes these negative associations, leading to feelings of self-dislike and animosity toward their autism. These negative tendencies are not set in stone, thankfully, but the journey toward self-acceptance can be long and arduous. Autistic people often express feelings of anger or disappointment regarding how their autism diagnosis was conveyed to them, in part because it left them feeling stigmatized and misunderstood. The journey is further complicated by societal attitudes and the lack of supportive environments that affirm the autistic identity. Understanding the impact of these initial disclosures and working toward a more positive and affirming approach can significantly improve the self-esteem and acceptance of autistic individuals.

Many autistic people report that the process of self-acceptance was prolonged because the negative perceptions of autism discouraged them from seeking information about it, or because they lacked access to adequate information from those around them. Without positive framing or comprehensive resources, these individuals often struggled to understand and embrace their identity. As a result, it was harder for them to recognize their strengths and build a positive self-image.

Many other autistic individuals report they had an easier path to self-acceptance because they had support groups, autism advocates, and educational resources. By connecting with others who shared similar experiences and by gaining access to positive representations of autism, they gradually learned to view their differences as strengths. Finding mentors or role models within the autistic community provided invaluable guidance and inspiration, showing that it is possible to lead a fulfilling and successful life as an autistic person. These resources and connections helped them dismantle internalized negative beliefs, which promoted a sense of pride and acceptance in their neurodivergent identity.

The stories of these individuals illuminate the importance of presenting an autism diagnosis to children in a positive way. When parents adopt a positive and informed approach, and provide supportive resources, children are more likely to develop a healthy self-image and embrace their autism at an earlier age.

Some of the best resources are children's books written to portray autism and other forms of neurodivergence in a truthful and positive way. Books can be valuable for initiating conversations about autism with any child, including allistic kids. When autism is presented in a positive light and accompanied by affirming information about neurodiversity, autistic individuals often develop a positive and accepting perspective of their autism. These books can help children understand and embrace their unique differences while also fostering acceptance and inclusivity among their peers. I have created a short reading list of potentially helpful books to assist children in understanding different kinds of minds. This reading list can be found in the appendix of this book.

In addition to children's books, there are many sources of information about autism for allistic adults, including research articles, blogs, videos, books, and other tools. These resources provide insights into the autistic experience and can help bridge the knowledge gap between autistic and allistic people. By taking the initiative to learn about autism, allistic individuals can better understand and support the autistic people in their lives. I have compiled a resource list, which can also be found in the appendix of the book.

I owe much of my progress toward self-acceptance to the accommodations, resources, and relational support that I received over the years. Believe me, getting the right support can feel like unlocking a hidden level in a video game. Everything just works better. I am immensely thankful for my friends, family members, supervisors, colleagues, lecturers, and managers who are receptive and well-informed about autism. They have provided the necessary support for my success, including the provision of online learning options, awareness of my communication requirements, and assistance in preparing for social interactions. So, whether it is a task list that saves my sanity or a friend who knows to give me a heads-up before plans change, these accommodations have made a world of difference.

Practical Strategies for Self-Disclosure

A positive disclosure experience can lead to understanding, acceptance, and access to support services and accommodations. Many autistic people, despite the risks I described earlier in the chapter, have a strong desire to share more about themselves with others. Disclosing the diagnosis can be a significant step toward self-acceptance and solidarity with the autistic community, a way for autistic people to embrace their identity and present themselves to the world on their own terms.

Emma felt so much better after she disclosed her diagnosis. She gained confidence to share openly about her experiences. Disclosure enabled her to feel part of a community that understood her. Nate now feels comfortable telling people he is autistic. Doing so gives him a sense of belonging and helps others understand him better. By disclosing their autism, autistic individuals often experience a deeper connection with the autistic community. Disclosure also helps them raise awareness about autism, disrupt stereotypes and misconceptions, and promote the acceptance of autistic people in schools and workplaces. The courageous openness of autistic people can create a ripple effect of understanding and inclusion.

All that being true, some individuals may choose not to disclose their diagnosis. This decision should be respected. No person should be forced to share information about themselves. Each person has the right to decide if and when they want to disclose their diagnosis. Autistic people might choose to share information with only a small group, such as their board of trustees, or they may prefer to wait before sharing with others.

When I was diagnosed, I chose to sit with the experience and my emotions, processing them on my own for a few months. This period of introspection felt important to me because I wanted to understand and manage my feelings without the added complexity of other people's emotions influencing my thoughts. I realized that involving others immediately would mean answering their questions and helping them process their reactions to my disclosure. This would have forced me to focus on others before myself, potentially preventing me from fully processing the experience on my terms. Having time for self-reflection allowed me to better understand my diagnosis and how it fit into my identity. After that period of personal reflection, I prepared scripts for what I would say and how I would answer potential questions. Then I disclosed my autism to one or two people at a time. This was my approach to disclosure, but it may not be right for everyone.

Despite the unique needs and preferences of each person, I believe there are some helpful strategies that all autistic people can use to help them disclose a diagnosis. These strategies do not apply to children, but they are helpful for most teenagers, young adults, and adults.

Being well-prepared before an important meeting or event always reduces stress. The same is true when you have decided to disclose an autism diagnosis. I recommend that you start with an outline of the main points you would like to share. Consider explaining how your autism manifests or what you hope to achieve

YOU, ME, AND AUTISM

by disclosing. For instance, you might say, "I wanted to share with you that I've been diagnosed as autistic. I'm sharing this because you're important to me, and I believe it will help deepen our understanding of each other." You may also want to express what the diagnosis means to you, such as, "This diagnosis has been instrumental in my journey of self-discovery, helping me understand myself better." Additionally, it is helpful to communicate any specific support needs or accommodations you may require. For example, you could say, "I find social interactions in crowded and noisy environments to be challenging. I'd prefer to have our gatherings in quieter settings."

These conversations often evolve over time as you discover more about your needs and preferences, and as those around you learn how best to support you. Think of it as an ongoing series, like your favorite TV show—always developing, always entertaining, but hopefully with fewer cliffhangers. By preparing a script before the conversation, you will be well-prepared to star in the most important role of your life: being authentically you.

While preparing for these discussions, it might be useful to anticipate the reactions of those who will hear the news. Then think about how you might respond to those reactions. Some people may have questions out of genuine curiosity, others might react with surprise, and others might need time to process the information. To respond to those who are sincerely curious and full of questions, you can be prepared with information that will help them learn about autism. You could also point them to reputable sources of information.

For those who receive the news about an autism diagnosis, it is important to never be dismissive of the autistic person who

Disclosure

shares such personal information. Engage in open conversations about how you can offer your autistic friend, coworker, or relative the best support. It is crucial to respect each person's experience and needs. In fact, I recommend that you conduct your own research rather than solely rely on the autistic individual for information about autism. As you study the issues, it is important to avoid false information that spreads around the internet and to find scholarly sources of information, such as from reputable autism associations and journals. This approach can demonstrate your commitment to understanding autism and being a part of a trusted support team.

And here is a final word of encouragement for parents. If you have recently completed the diagnostic process with your child, I recommend that you allow yourself time to process the information and be kind to yourself. The diagnostic journey can be emotionally taxing, so it is important to give yourself grace.

CHAPTER 9

Symphony of Life

Human existence, individually and collectively, requires us to orchestrate our lives in a way that enables us to meet our basic needs. These needs must be met for us to have a healthy and fulfilled life. The work of meeting these needs is akin to a symphony that supports the grand composition of overall well-being. In my view, the elements of this symphony involve eating and drinking, sleep, personal hygiene, and home maintenance.

Consider first the importance of nourishment. The ingestion of food and drink serves as a sacred communion between body and sustenance, fueling the vessel for each day's endeavors. Proper nutrition provides energy, fortifies the body against ailments, and enhances cognitive function. And there is nothing quite like the existential joy of a perfectly baked pizza slice.

Then there is the element of sleep, the nighttime phase when weary souls find respite, bodies rejuvenate, dreams whisper secrets of the subconscious, and hearts are prepared for the challenges that await in the dawn's embrace. For some, if you are like me, sleep is upended by hours of tossing and turning while my mind ponders the mysteries of the universe. Insomnia can disrupt the symphony because sleep is essential for maintaining mental health, emotional balance, and physical vitality.

Personal hygiene, the rituals of cleansing and bodily care, defends the harmony of our lives against the cacophony of illness and affliction. Hygiene preserves the sanctity of the human form and contributes to overall well-being by preventing disease and fostering a sense of self-respect and confidence.

Home, a sanctuary in its own right, is where the humble acts of housework transcend mere chores. Caring for our homes involves rituals of reverence for the spaces we inhabit. Maintaining a clean and orderly home safeguards us against decay and malady, providing a stable foundation for daily life, mental clarity, and peace.

Like a symphony, we need to orchestrate our daily efforts to create a melody of health and happiness. To neglect any element of the symphony is to risk discord in the grand composition of life. It is incumbent on us to honor these needs, for in their fulfilment we experience a well-lived life and create a positive ripple effect that extends to those around us.

Unfortunately, autistic individuals often encounter numerous obstacles that make it harder for them to conduct the symphony, which could lead to a decline in physical and mental well-being. Most people conduct the orchestra of self-care like a maestro, but autistic people struggle to overcome sensory overload, dietary restrictions, and sleep disruptions.

Eating and Drinking

Consumption of food and drink presents numerous challenges for autistic individuals. Some people struggle to make decisions about what to consume and how to prepare meals, which can feel like a multilevel quest with plot twists! Autistic individuals, because of interoceptive differences, do not always recognize when they are hungry or thirsty. This can lead to inconsistent eating patterns and

Symphony of Life

nutritional deficiencies. Imagine your stomach trying to send you an "I am hungry" email that keeps getting stuck in the spam folder. The sensory aspects of food, such as texture, taste, and smell, can also pose significant obstacles, resulting in a limited diet. Additionally, executive functioning challenges can make it difficult to plan and prepare meals, often leading to reliance on familiar, easily accessible foods that may not be nutritionally balanced.

Our interoceptive sense plays a crucial role in signaling hunger. However, many autistic individuals do not perceive or interpret these signals accurately, which leads to uncertainty about when to eat. To manage this challenge, it helps me to set reminder alarms or to receive support from friends or family members. These strategies help establish a more consistent eating schedule, ensuring that nutritional needs are met even when internal hunger cues are not easily recognized. Mealtime routines can be more positive when autistic people respect their unique sensory preferences and food aversions. Most people just get hungry and eat, but for autistic people to eat well, they need to choreograph mealtimes with careful planning, tech support, and help from friends or relatives.

Moreover, when autistic individuals are engrossed in an enjoyable activity, such as a special interest, it can be difficult for them to attend to meal preparation. Many autistic individuals experience hyperfocus, characterized by prolonged and intense concentration on a particular subject or task. Hyperfocus enabled me to write this entire book in six weeks while simultaneously pursuing a PhD and managing a randomized control trial of a new support program for autistic children—without compromising the quality of any work. Hyperfocus is a unique aspect of my autism that allows me to accomplish great things. However, this intense focus comes with a cost. It negatively affects the quantity and regularity of my sleep and eating habits. Hyperfocus leads me to say to myself, *Who needs food or sleep when I am in the zone?* This is an unhealthy but common experience for many autistic individuals.

I also experience something known as *autistic inertia.* This term refers to the difficulty of initiating or ceasing activities, as well as transitioning from one task to another. Even when I am not engaged in anything particularly captivating, my brain will not let me stand up and walk to the kitchen. I might be internally screaming at myself to act, but my brain and body remain unresponsive. This experience is deeply frustrating, defies logic, contradicts my desires, and feels like being trapped in a trance. Autistic inertia is not procrastination or laziness; it is a genuine struggle with task initiation and transition. It can affect many aspects of life, from daily routines to critical tasks.

Establishing predictable routines can serve as an effective coping mechanism for managing hyperfocus and autistic inertia. Adhering to a set schedule fosters a sense of control and stability. Structured routines can mitigate the effects of autistic inertia and facilitate the transition out of hyperfocus. To maintain consistency, I created a schedule, laminated it, and placed it on my fridge. A laminated schedule allows me to use a whiteboard marker to cross off each item once completed, providing a visual and tactile sense of accomplishment. (If you need an example, you can download my morning schedule for free at: https://mymorningroutine.tiiny. site/.) In addition, it can help to use transition notifications and to set allotted times for each task. On some days I can seamlessly shift from one activity to the next, but on other days, even with the same routine, I might struggle.

The "tendril theory" illustrates the complexity faced by autistic

Symphony of Life

people when making transitions. According to this theory, our minds extend countless "tendrils" of thought when we are engrossed in a task. Each tendril connects to various thoughts and emotions. When we switch tasks, the tendrils must be retracted. Abrupt interruptions or sudden transitions can feel like the tendrils are being forcibly torn away, which can be distressing and disorienting. Sudden transitions disrupt the flow of thoughts and emotions that had been harmoniously connected to the previous activity.

When given adequate time to proceed through a transition, autistic individuals can retract mental tendrils at a slower pace, which helps them stay regulated. Therefore, it is crucial to provide autistic people with transition warnings and sufficient time to mentally prepare for an upcoming change, reducing the likelihood of stress and dysregulation. Implementing consistent routines and using visual aids or written reminders can also help.

All these factors affect the process of deciding what to eat. When confronted with endless food and recipe choices, autistic people can easily become overwhelmed, possibly leading to a shutdown. When faced with a plethora of options, I often retreat into a state of indecision. I say to myself, *I don't want to eat anymore.* When I am paralyzed with meal decisions, well-intentioned allistic people might bombard me with questions or choices, which exacerbates the situation. Who knew that deciding between toast and pizza could feel like choosing a Hogwarts house?

Research indicates that when autistic people are presented with many choices, they are more inclined to select either the first or last option. This helps them to promptly conclude an overwhelming scenario. Therefore, it is usually best to offer only two options that are known to be among the autistic person's food preferences. If no one is present to assist, autistic people can write out a list of top food choices (use pictures if that is helpful) and display it on the fridge or nearby in the kitchen. This approach can alleviate decision-making stress and streamline meal selection. Once food is stored in the pantry or fridge, autistic people often forget about it. Out of sight, out of mind—literally. Keeping visible reminders of which preferred foods are available can ensure that meals are less stressful to select.

It can also be helpful to provide choices well in advance, allowing ample time for consideration. For instance, discussing meal options the day before gives the autistic individual time to process the choices without the pressure of immediate decision-making. Creating a weekly meal plan can also be beneficial, as it reduces the frequency of decisions and establishes a predictable routine.

Then there is the challenge of meal preparation. For me and many other autistic individuals, the process of making a meal can seem overwhelming. Take, for instance, the seemingly straightforward task of brewing a cup of tea. It involves filling the kettle with water, boiling the water, retrieving a mug from the cupboard, choosing a type of tea, and choosing whether to add water or milk first. All that might seem simple, but for me those steps can seem like quantum physics. My brain tries to process all the steps at once as if it were trying to open forty-seven tabs in a browser simultaneously. Making a meal requires far more choices and steps than making tea. Sometimes I look at the kitchen and think, *Maybe I'll just eat air today. It's a low-calorie and low-effort meal.* While others breeze through culinary endeavors, I am negotiating peace treaties with tea bags.

Many autistic individuals grapple with prioritizing tasks. Consequently, when our brains encounter a barrage of steps, we find

Symphony of Life

ourselves unable to discern priorities amidst the chaos, leading to a state of paralysis. Cognitive overload can make meal preparation appear daunting, resulting in the avoidance of the task altogether.

As a result, I seldom prepare what might be deemed a traditional meal. Instead, I often choose the culinary equivalent of a speed-dating session: reheating premade dishes, munching on snacks, or whipping up a gourmet creation like pasta with butter and cheese. This might deviate from conventional culinary norms, but it is important to recognize that consuming something, even if it is a modest meal, is preferable to surviving on air. Simplifying meal preparation can ensure that nutritional needs are met without overwhelming the individual. Preparing bulk meals in advance and freezing portions for later use can also be an effective strategy. It can help to incorporate nutritional supplements or fortified foods to fill dietary gaps, ensuring that basic nutritional needs are met even when meals are simple. Flexible meal planning and unconventional eating habits are valid ways to improve health for autistic individuals.

As I mentioned earlier, I gravitate toward what is colloquially known as a beige diet, which means that I typically avoid fruits and vegetables. This dietary preference can hinder adequate nutrition.

Two other strategies can be helpful: ABC shopping and rainbow shopping. ABC shopping involves finding foods that start with the next letter of the alphabet. For example, A is for apple or avocado, B is for banana or biscuits, and C is for cucumber or croquettes. This makes shopping seem like a culinary scavenger hunt! Using a game-like approach can make shopping more enjoyable and might even lead to delightful discoveries. The second strategy, rainbow shopping, involves finding foods in the colors of the rainbow. For instance, red foods include apples, strawberries, and Kit Kats (the red wrapper totally counts); orange foods include carrots, oranges, and cheese; and yellow foods include pasta, bananas, and lemons. These methods also make the shopping experience more enjoyable, and they ensure a diverse intake of nutrients by incorporating a wide range of colorful fruits and vegetables. Plus, you get the bonus of looking like a walking, talking rainbow at the checkout counter. Taste the rainbow—literally!

It is still important to consider individual sensory needs. By gradually incorporating small amounts of new foods, autistic people can diversify dietary preferences without overwhelming the senses. For instance, blending fruits and vegetables into sauces or smoothies allows for the incorporation of healthy ingredients in a less intrusive way. Autistic people might be open to experimenting with different textures and flavors to find what works best.

I have a strong aversion to food items touching each other on the plate. Traditional plates and bowls do not prevent food from mixing. It helps to use specialized dinnerware with partitions that keep food separated in designated areas. This simple accommodation makes the dining experience much more comfortable, reducing the sensory overload that can occur when different foods mix. I, for one, do not want my mashed potatoes mingling with my green beans without permission. I prefer to let each food shine on a stage of its own. Bravo!

The information provided above does not constitute nutritional advice. If you have any medical concerns, you should consult with a general practitioner or a qualified nutritionist.

Sleeping

Sleep is an essential element of overall well-being. Unfortunately, autistic individuals frequently experience sleep difficulties caused by heightened anxiety, sensory challenges, and a need for more sleep than allistic individuals. Autistic people have higher rates of insomnia, staying asleep, and achieving REM sleep. Research indicates that between 50 percent and 80 percent of autistic people struggle with sleep, compared to about 20 percent to 30 percent of allistic people. This disparity is astounding.

Autistic individuals usually have intense struggles with anxiety due to the numerous challenges we face in everyday life. Anxiety can make it difficult for us to relax and quiet our minds, which often results in prolonged periods of trying to fall asleep. Research suggests that it typically takes autistic people longer than twenty minutes to fall asleep. For many, it can take several hours. I often find myself lying in bed until the early morning while trying to calm my racing thoughts. Similarly, Helen often stays awake due to racing thoughts. Long delays in falling asleep can exacerbate anxiety and further disrupt sleep patterns, contributing to a cycle of sleeplessness and increased stress. The lack of sleep then affects daytime functioning, leading to even more anxiety and difficulty managing daily tasks.

To manage nighttime anxiety, I try to make my evenings as relaxing as possible. I create a calming evening routine, which sends a signal to the body that it is time to wind down. Establishing consistent pre-sleep rituals, such as reading, taking a warm bath, or practicing meditation, can be beneficial. Both Sam and I enjoy listening to white noise and rain sounds, which can help us relax and calm our minds. We also like autonomous sensory meridian response (ASMR), which refers to the tingling sensation during a gentle whisper or a head massage. I like to call it "brain tickles." I also avoid anxiety-provoking topics in the evening. By postponing big discussions about stressful subjects until daytime, I prevent the activation of stress responses that can keep me awake at night. I never debate the existence of aliens or discuss the mysteries of the universe right before bed, otherwise I am up all night pondering life's greatest questions. Keep it light, keep it calm, and drift off into dreamland with ease. Limiting evening social interactions, which can be stressful for autistic people, can also be helpful.

In some cases, autistic people could consult a medical professional about sleep medications. Medication can be helpful, but it is important to get professional advice about your situation and to ensure that side effects are managed properly. There are also non-pharmaceutical interventions, such as cognitive-behavioral therapy for insomnia (CBT-I), that might address the underlying causes of sleep disturbances.

For autistic people, sensitivities to light, sound, and touch can become significant barriers against falling asleep and staying asleep. Sensory stimuli can divert the brain's focus away from relaxation, making it challenging to achieve restful sleep. For instance, when sunlight enters my room, I wake up immediately and cannot fall asleep again. It is like the sun has a personal vendetta against my beauty sleep. This issue is particularly pronounced during the summer when daylight hours are extended, resulting in reduced overall sleep duration. After years of waking up early as a child, my parents invested in blackout curtains for my benefit and theirs. Blackout curtains are an excellent solution for minimizing light exposure and creating a darker, more conducive sleep environment. Eye masks can block out light that may seep in from other sources.

Sam discussed how using his computer before bed makes it harder for him to fall asleep. Research shows that blue light from screens, including televisions, and increased mental stimulation from computer and video content can cause insomnia. Sam tries to avoid screens before going to sleep. So, draw those blackout curtains, don your eye mask, and bid goodnight to your screens. A sleep sanctuary awaits!

Each of us has a circadian rhythm, the natural cycle of feeling awake or sleepy. Our circadian rhythm plays a crucial role in regulating sleep patterns, but it is influenced by natural cycles of light and dark. Autistic individuals' heightened sensitivity to light may curtail their exposure to sunlight, potentially dampening the influence of natural cues on circadian rhythms, thereby complicating the process of falling asleep.

To address these sensory challenges, in addition to the strategies mentioned above, autistic people can benefit from comfortable bedding materials and sleepwear that do not irritate the skin. Some people prefer weighted blankets or compression sheets for the calming effect they provide. Some individuals might need a cooler room, whereas others prefer a warmer environment.

The rapid eye movement (REM) sleep stage is crucial for processing emotions and memories, as well as for restoring the brain and body. Research indicates that autistic people spend about 15 percent of their sleep in the REM stage compared to approximately 25 percent for allistic individuals. Consequently, autistic people often need to sleep longer to achieve the same amount of restorative REM sleep as allistic people. I have always preferred to go to bed early. In fact, I have been teased for being "born a grandma" because I require so much sleep to function properly. Emma shared similar experiences. She is easily fatigued and needs more hours of sleep. She knows that if she does not go to sleep early, she will struggle to function well the next day. Emma has found that managing her schedule to ensure she gets sufficient sleep is crucial for maintaining her well-being and daily productivity. Allistic people should accept the fact that most autistic people need more sleep. Our bodies and brains need extra rest to function at their best.

Sleep also plays a crucial role in restoring the immune system, regulating moods, processing memories and emotions, boosting memory and concentration, releasing growth hormones for body growth and repair, and conserving energy for the following day. Autistic and allistic people should make the sanctuary of sleep a top priority in life.

Personal Hygiene

Personal hygiene is crucial for preventing the spread of illnesses and avoiding infections. This includes dental, body, hair, and hand and nail hygiene. Too little focus on personal hygiene can lead to an infected cut or the transmission of illness. Too much focus on personal hygiene might lead someone to wear down the enamel on their teeth or to scrub their skin raw.

Autistic individuals may face challenges with personal hygiene due to sensory and communication differences, and difficulty making transitions. To some autistic people, toothpaste feels like sandpaper, which discourages them from brushing. Many autistic people say that when they wash their hair the water feels like a million tiny needles. Basic hygiene can feel like a spa day gone wrong. Other autistic people tend to go overboard with personal hygiene, turning basic self-care into an extreme sport.

Sensory differences can complicate hygiene routines, often because many cleaning tasks involve water. Some autistic individuals may dislike the sensation of water and prefer using a wet flannel for cleaning. Others might have thermal sensitivities, requiring water to be significantly colder or hotter than what is typically comfortable for allistic people. Thermal sensitivities can significantly impact comfort levels during tasks such as washing hands, showering, or brushing teeth. For example, some individuals may find lukewarm water soothing, while others may need very cold or very hot water to feel comfortable. Goldilocks had nothing on us when it comes to getting the temperature "just right." Additionally, certain soaps and cleaning products might have overwhelming scents. For those who are sensitive to strong smells, fragrance-free soaps, shampoos, and lotions can be a better choice. Some individuals might prefer products with specific textures, such as creamy, gel-based, or foamy formulations. These preferences can vary widely and may change over time.

Maintaining a sensory record can provide valuable long-term insights. By recording reactions to various sensory inputs during hygiene routines, patterns can emerge that highlight specific triggers or preferences. This strategy helps autistic people to becoming sensory detectives. Sherlock Holmes would be proud! You can search for ways to make hygiene routines less of a battle and more of a breeze. As you develop the sensory record, you can keep a couple of questions in mind: Do you have sensory sensitivities to water, texture, or sound that impact your personal hygiene routine? Do the tools or products you use to assist with personal hygiene help or hurt your efforts?

As previously discussed, autistic individuals often struggle with transitioning from one activity to another, which the tendril theory explains. Therefore, autistic people set aside unenjoyable personal hygiene necessities to stay focused on activities they enjoy. Visual cues can be beneficial in such instances. Creating a personal hygiene schedule with pictures can help autistic people remember the need for regular self-care. Timers and alarms can provide auditory cues to signal the end of one activity and the start of another, helping to ease transitions. Using a strategy of gradual adjustments can also make the process smoother.

Autistic and allistic individuals often face communication differences that can impact how personal hygiene tasks are learned and understood. Typically, hygiene instruction is conveyed verbally; however, autistic individuals often struggle to remember instructions delivered through verbal communication alone. This difficulty can result in the incorrect completion of hygiene tasks or the avoidance of them altogether. To address these challenges, it is beneficial to use a variety of communication methods to ensure clear understanding. Visual cues, such as charts, step-by-step picture guides, or social stories can offer precise instructions and help an autistic person to divide tasks into manageable steps. Demonstrations can help autistic individuals observe proper techniques and ask questions.

Autistic individuals often feel overwhelmed by all the steps required to complete a simple task. For example, allistic people will only think about brushing their teeth as a single task, but autistic people will think about all the steps leading up to, during, and after brushing their teeth: standing up, walking to the bathroom, locating the toothbrush and toothpaste, applying the toothpaste, brushing, rinsing, and putting the items back where they belong. For autistic people, thinking about all these steps can be overwhelming.

So, autistic people need to focus on one step at a time. Doing so will transform a daunting mountain climb into a series of gentle hills. Using visual aids, such as checklists or picture guides, can help autistic people to track progress through each step, providing a sense of accomplishment and reducing anxiety. Who does not love checking boxes and feeling like a champion at the end of a routine? Gold star for brushing those pearly whites!

When I was younger, my parents taught me a toothbrushing song to make the process more enjoyable. I still sing it today. It is a chart-topper in my personal playlist. "Brush, brush, brush your teeth, brush your teeth with glee. Brush brush brush, brush brush brush, brush your teeth with me." Incorporating fun with hygiene tasks can make them more manageable. Watching YouTube, listening to music, or having a favorite item nearby can provide comfort and motivation. Sometimes, a little dance party with your toothbrush is just what you need. This multifaceted approach can transform personal hygiene tasks into enjoyable and achievable routines.

For autistic women and teenage girls, managing menstruation can be challenging. Periods introduce a change to our usual personal care routine, and this disruption can be difficult to navigate. It can also be hard to talk about. Discussing periods is sometimes avoided or considered taboo, but it is essential to address this natural bodily function as part of personal care.

The additional tasks that come with menstruation, such as using sanitary products, monitoring the cycle, showering regularly, and managing discomfort or pain, can add layers of complexity to female personal care routines. Dividing these tasks into manageable steps, using visual aids, and setting reminders can keep everything on track. Maintaining personal hygiene during each period will ensure cleanliness and comfort. Regular showers prevent bacterial buildup, reduce the risk of odors, and provide a refreshing break. Changing sanitary products frequently and wearing breathable, clean underwear also contributes to maintaining hygiene.

Many autistic females might forget to change their sanitary products regularly, which can lead to health issues and discomfort. Sensory issues often reduce the motivation to change them. For example, some autistic women or teenage girls might have an aversion to the smell of blood, causing them to delay changing their products. On the other hand, some may need to maintain a consistent sensory experience, in which case they might feel compelled to change their pad frequently to avoid any change in texture. There are many types of menstrual products, including disposable and washable pads, tampons, and menstrual cups. Each should be used according to the product's instructions. Medical professionals can provide counsel when needed. In addition, autistic females can better manage periods by experimenting with different menstruation products to find what feels most comfortable and least disruptive.

I encourage autistic females to have open discussions about periods with trusted individuals or health care professionals. Books, videos, and workshops can help everyone learn about period management. Downloading a period tracking app can be useful, but some might prefer to mark period dates in a personal diary or calendar, which improves privacy. Combining these methods can provide multiple prompts, ensuring proper period management. When you notice that your period is near, it can be helpful to carry extra underwear and menstruation products in your bag. This preparation ensures that you are not caught by surprise and can manage your period comfortably even when you are away from home.

Managing periods can be a part of life for up to forty years or more. This journey involves understanding personal preferences, addressing sensory sensitivities, and ensuring that the chosen products meet the individual's unique requirements.

Home Maintenance

Home maintenance is a crucial aspect of daily life, ensuring we have clean clothes, dishes, food, and a safe environment. However, the sensory difficulties and executive functioning challenges of autistic individuals can make housework seem daunting. A pile of dirty laundry might look like an unscalable mountain. Fortunately, there are many strategies, including those already discussed, that can help make housework more manageable for autistic people.

Sensory difficulties can significantly impact an autistic person's ability to deal with home maintenance. Many cleaning products have strong or overpowering scents, leading to sensory overload. My aversion to contact with water makes cleaning more difficult. To address this, I use long-handled cleaning tools that allow me to avoid direct contact with water. I imagine I am wielding a mighty sword of cleanliness from a safe distance. Wearing gloves or using cleaning wipes can also reduce sensory overload and make cleaning more manageable.

Beyond the struggle with sensory overload, autistic people face executive functioning challenges that significantly impact home maintenance tasks. For example, executive function limitations and sensory differences can disrupt supermarket shopping. I addressed this aspect of life earlier, in the context of nutrition, but going to the supermarket is also a central aspect of home management. We need to decide on a meal plan, make a shopping list, and figure out a food budget. I find it helpful to ask someone for assistance with all these needs, which reduces the likelihood of feeling overwhelmed once I get to the store.

Driving to the store can be stressful, particularly during peak traffic times, adding to the overall anxiety of the task. Entering the supermarket often means confronting a barrage of sensory stimuli: crowded aisles, loud music, bright lights, and colorful marketing materials. This environment can quickly lead to sensory overload. It can help to use noise-cancelling headphones or to bring along a support person. Think of your support person as a supermarket safari guide, leading you through the jungle of discounts and delis.

To avoid trips to the supermarket, I often have my groceries delivered. I sometimes request market staff to gather my items ahead of time so that I can pick them up without entering the store. And on some occasions, I ask a support person to shop for me or accompany me during nonpeak hours. During less busy times, my local supermarket offers a sensory-friendly hour when they dim the lights and turn off the music. When I need to pick up an item myself, I go to the store during quieter times and wear noise-cancelling headphones. To stay focused on my objective amidst the overwhelming sensory input, I repeat the name of the item I need in my mind, such as "butter, butter, butter" as a mantra, which helps me stay focused in the chaos of the dairy aisle.

Large cleaning tasks, such as tidying a room or scrubbing the bathroom, can also feel overwhelming and trigger anxiety. I often stare at Mount Laundry and wonder if I should bring more snacks for the climb. The immense number of required steps to conquer the job makes it difficult to prioritize and determine where to begin. However, I have a strategy that helps: using visual cleaning schedules. These schedules divide the overall job into manageable sections, a step by step approach. By presenting the subtasks in a visual format, the job becomes less daunting and more structured. I complement the visual schedule by allocating specific time slots for each task and using a timer. You can find examples of two visual schedules that I created, one for cleaning a room and another for cleaning a bathroom, at these links: https://cleaningyourroom.tiiny.site/ and https://cleaningyourbathroom.tiiny.site/.

Overall, autistic people can simplify housework by establishing a consistent routine. I have a weekly schedule that designates specific housework tasks to certain days. Every Tuesday I clean the bathroom, and every Sunday I clean my room and do the laundry. By distributing these tasks throughout the week, I can take breaks and avoid mental fatigue. Writing my routine in a schedule helps me stay organized and ensures that I tackle housework in manageable chunks.

These strategies, which work for me, can be customized to fit individual sensory preferences and executive functioning variations. By encouraging autistic people to design their own methods for eating, sleep, personal hygiene, and house maintenance, they can orchestrate a beautiful symphony of life that is fulfilling, manageable, and safe. They will gain a sense of self-control and independence, and they will be better equipped to navigate daily challenges and thrive in personal and communal spaces.

Epilogue

While writing *You, Me, and Autism*, I found myself reflecting on the incredible diversity and resilience within the autistic community. Writing the book was a deeply personal and transformative experience. The process of bringing this book to life opened my eyes to the myriad ways that autism is experienced and understood, revealing the rich tapestry of stories that make up the autistic community. Sam, Emma, Helen, Nate, and so many others have infused this book with their authenticity, courage, and uniqueness. Their willingness to share their lives with such honesty has illuminated the profound strength and individuality that defines autistic experiences. Each story has enriched the book and broadened my appreciation for what it means to be autistic. I have seen resilience in the face of adversity, joy in moments of triumph, and an unwavering sense of identity that shines through despite societal barriers.

Writing the book also reinforced my belief that acceptance and understanding are essential for a healthy society. I hope the practical strategies and insights offered in the book will help everyone cultivate a more compassionate and supportive world. By embracing neurodiversity, we can all learn to value and celebrate the differences that make each person so amazing and unique. Everyone can help create a world where all people, regardless of their neurological makeup, can thrive and be appreciated for who they are. Hopefully the personal stories, research, and practical tools in this book will help readers build bridges of empathy and understanding between allistic and autistic individuals. I hope that we all envision a future in which inclusivity is the norm rather than the exception.

Although I did not devote a full chapter to the topic, I want to emphasize the importance of humor in forging strong relationships between autistic and allistic people. Humor can make complex topics more approachable, reminding us that even in serious discussions, there is a place for joy and laughter. Humor has a unique power to create connections that transcend our differences. It can also promote empathy. Humor can serve as a vital counterbalance to weighty subjects, offering moments of relief and perspective. By using humor thoughtfully, we can navigate and process the multifaceted experiences of autism with a lighter heart. We should recognize and respect the gravity of autism-related topics, but humor can illuminate the human side of every story. It breaks down barriers, inviting everyone—regardless of their background or experience—to join in the conversation with openness and curiosity. It can turn the mundane into the memorable, and it can transform challenges into opportunities for growth and connection. Through humor, we can find common ground in the absurdities of life and remind ourselves that it is okay to smile, laugh, and find joy.

Looking ahead, I am filled with hope and optimism for the future. The conversations around autism and neurodiversity are evolving, becoming richer and more inclusive with each passing day. I believe we are moving toward a future in which we will celebrate differences and in which every individual is valued for their unique contributions. In that future, diverse ways of thinking and experiencing the world will be seen as strengths that enrich our communities.

However, there is still work to be done. Creating a society that embraces and celebrates all kinds of minds will require ongoing

Epilogue

commitment, education, and advocacy from each of us. It will take a collective effort to break down the barriers of misunderstanding and prejudice, and to build bridges of empathy and respect. Together, I believe we can achieve this vision.

I hope you carry with you a deeper understanding of the beautiful uniqueness in each person. May this book inspire you to advocate for acceptance, offer support, and spread awareness. We can all advocate for inclusive workplaces and schools. We can educate people about neurodiversity. We can support autistic individuals in our communities. Every small action contributes to the larger movement. Each conversation, each act of kindness, and each effort to learn and grow brings us closer to a society in which everyone feels valued and included. The story does not end here; it continues with each of us, every day, making a difference in the lives of those around us.

Acknowledgements

I am immensely grateful to everyone who contributed to this book. To the autistic individuals who shared their stories, thank you for your bravery and openness. Your willingness to share your personal experiences has provided invaluable insights and enriched the narrative with authenticity and depth. Your voices are the heart of this book, and your courage to share your journey is inspiring.

To the researchers and advocates who constantly work to better understand autism and to improve support for autistic people, your effort is invaluable. Your dedication to advancing knowledge and creating a more inclusive world for autistic individuals is a beacon of hope for many. Your efforts lay the groundwork for a future in which acceptance and support are the norm. Your contributions have profoundly impacted this book and the broader community.

To my dearest family and friends, your unwavering encouragement and support have been my strength. Your belief in me and this project has been a constant source of motivation and reassurance. Your patience, love, and understanding have made this journey possible. I am deeply thankful for your presence in my life. Each of you has played a crucial role in bringing this book to life, and for that, I am eternally grateful.

About the Author

Phoebe Jordan is an autistic researcher whose PhD work at Victoria University in Wellington, New Zealand, in partnership with researchers at Stanford University, focused on developing neurodiversity-affirming measures to evaluate the effectiveness of support efforts for autistic children.

Jordan's research has been published in *Autism, Lancet Regional Health Western Pacific,* and other major academic journals. She frequently presents her academic work at major conferences, on webinars, and at workshops. As an autistic woman and scholar, she contributes unique insights into the myriad talents, difficulties, and needs of other autistic individuals.

Jordan, who lives in New Zealand, also writes children's books designed to help young readers understand and express their emotions, and that celebrate neurodiversity and promote broader understanding and acceptance of different kinds of minds. For regular updates about Dr. Jordan, her scholarly work, and her other books, please visit upriverpress.com.

Appendix

Resources for Children

These ten books will introduce children to autism and other neurodivergences.

- *When my Brain is Messy* by Tania Wieclaw
- *Susie Spins* by Emma Dalmayne
- *The Little Senses* series by Samantha Cotterill
- *A Day With No Words* by Tiffany Hammond
- *The Big Umbrella* by Amy Bates and Juniper Bates
- *I Am an Autistic Girl* by Danuta Bulhak-Paterson
- *A First Look at Autism: I See Things Differently* by Pat Thomas and Claire Keay
- *The Brain Forest* by Sandhya Menon
- *Some Brains* by Nelly Thomas
- *Just Right For You* by Melanie Heyworth

Resources for Adults

These ten books will help adults better understand autism and other neurodivergences.

- *The Spectrum Girl's Survival Guide: How to Grow Up Awesome and Autistic* by Siena Castellon
- *Unmasking Autism* by Devon Price

- *Sincerely, Your Autistic Child* by Emily Paige Ballou
- *Taking Off the Mask: Practical Exercises to Help Understand and Minimize the Effects of Autistic Camouflaging* by Hannah Belcher
- *Women on the Spectrum: A Handbook for Life* by Emma Goodall and Yenn Purkis
- *The Nine Degrees of Autism: A Developmental Model for the Alignment and Reconciliation of Hidden Neurological Conditions* by Philip Wylie, Wenn Lawson, and Luke Beardon
- *Life and Love: Positive Strategies for Autistic Adults* by Zosia Zaks
- *The Neurodiverse Workplace: An Employer's Guide to Managing and Working with Neurodivergent Employees, Clients and Customers* by Victoria Honeybourne
- *Communicating Better with People on the Autism Spectrum* by Paddy-Joe Morgan
- *I Am Autistic* by Chanelle Moriah

Bibliography

Accardo, Jennifer. "Food Selectivity in Autism: Expanding the Palate (and Palette)." *The Journal of Pediatrics* 211, (2019): 1-3. https://doi.org/10.1016/j.jpeds.2019.06.007.

Alaghband-rad, Javan, et al. "Camouflage and Masking Behavior in Adult Autism." *Frontiers in Psychiatry 14,* (2023). https://doi.org/10.3389/fpsyt.2023.1108110.

Anderson, Connie, et al. "Young Adults on the Autism Spectrum and Early Employment-Related Experiences: Aspirations and Obstacles." *Journal of Autism and Developmental Disorders* 51, no. 1 (2020): 88-105. https://doi.org/10.1007/s10803-020-04513-4.

Anderson-Chavarria, Melissa. "The Autism Predicament: Models of Autism and Their Impact on Autistic Identity." *Disability & Society 37,* no. 8 (2021): 1321-1341. https://doi.org/10.1080/09687599.2021.1877117.

Ashforth, Blake and Beth Schinoff. "Identity Under Construction: How Individuals Come to Define Themselves in Organizations." *Annual Review of Organizational Psychology and Organizational Behavior* 3, no. 1 (2016): 111-137. https://doi.org/10.1146/annurev-orgpsych-041015-062322.

Bagatell, Nancy. "Orchestrating Voices: Autism, Identity and the Power of Discourse." *Disability & Society* 22, no. 4 (2007): 413-426. https://doi.org/10.1080/09687590701337967.

Baranek, Grace, et al. "Sensory Experiences Questionnaire: Discriminating Sensory Features in Young Children with Autism, Developmental Delays, and Typical Development." *Journal of Child Psychology and Psychiatry* 47, no. 6 (2006): 591-601. https://doi.org/10.1111/j.1469-7610.2005.01546.x.

Belek, Ben. "Articulating Sensory Sensitivity: From Bodies with Autism to Autistic Bodies." *Medical Anthropology* 38, no. 1 (2018): 30-43. https://doi.org/10.1080/01459740.2018.1460750.

Benevides, Teal, et al. "Listening to the Autistic Voice: Mental Health Priorities to Guide Research and Practice in Autism from a Stakeholder-Driven Project." *Autism* 24, no. 4 (2020): 822-833. https://doi.org/10.1177/1362361320908410.

Black, Melissa, et al. "Experiences of Friendships for Individuals on the Autism Spectrum: A Scoping Review." *Review Journal of Autism and Developmental Disorders* 11, no. 1 (2022): 184-209. https://doi.org/10.1007/s40489-022-00332-8.

Blanche, Emma Imperatore, et al. "Proprioceptive Processing Difficulties among Children with Autism Spectrum Disorders and Developmental Disabilities." *The American Journal of Occupational Therapy* 66, no. 5 (2012): 621-624. https://doi.org/10.5014/ajot.2012.004234.

Boldsen, Sophie. "Autism and the Sensory Disruption of Social Experience." *Frontiers in Psychology* 13, (2022). https://doi.org/10.3389/fpsyg.2022.874268.

Bosman, Renate and Jochem Thijs. "Language Preferences in the Dutch Autism Community: A Social Psychological Approach." *Journal of Autism and Developmental Disorders* 54, no. 5 (2023): 1727-1739. https://doi.org/10.1007/s10803-023-05903-0.

Botha, Monique, et al. "Does Language Matter? Identity-First Versus Person-First Language Use in Autism Research: A Response to Vivanti." Center for Open Science. OSFPreprints (2020). https://doi.org/10.31219/osf.io/75n83.

Bradley, Louise, et al. "Autistic Adults' Experiences of Camouflaging and Its Perceived Impact on Mental Health." *Autism in Adulthood* 3, no. 4 (2021): 320-329. https://doi.org/10.1089/aut.2020.0071.

Bradshaw, Pia, et al. "'Autistic' or 'with Autism'? Why the Way General Practitioners View and Talk about Autism Matters." *Australian Journal of General Practice* 50, no. 3 (2021): 104-108. https://doi.org/10.31128/ajgp-11-20-5721.

Bross, Leslie Ann, et al. "Examining the Special Interest Areas of Autistic Adults with a Focus on Their Employment and Mental Health Outcomes." *Journal of Vocational Rehabilitation* 57, no. 3 (2022): 289-305. https://doi.org/10.3233/jvr-221218.

Buckle, Karen, et al. "'No Way Out Except from External Intervention'": First-Hand Accounts of Autistic Inertia." Center for Open Science. PsyArXiv Preprints. (2020). https://doi.org/10.31234/osf.io/ahk6x.

Bury, Simon, et al. "Understanding Language Preference: Autism Knowledge, Experience of Stigma and Autism Identity." *Autism 27,* no. 6 (2022): 1588-1600. https://doi.org/10.1177/13623613221142383.

Butera, Christiana, et al. "Relationships between Alexithymia, Interoception, and Emotional Empathy in Autism Spectrum Disorder." *Autism* 27, no. 3 (2022): 690-703. https://doi.org/10.1177/13623613221111310.

Cage, Eilidh and Zoe Troxell-Whitman. "Understanding the Relationships between Autistic Identity, Disclosure, and Camouflaging." *Autism in Adulthood* 2, no. 4 (2020): 334-338. https://doi.org/10.1089/aut.2020.0016.

Cage, Eilidh, et al. "Experiences of Autism Acceptance and Mental Health in Autistic Adults." *Journal of Autism and Developmental Disorders* 48, no. 2 (2017): 473-484. https://doi.org/10.1007/s10803-017-3342-7.

Cappadocia, M. Catherine, et al. "Bullying Experiences among Children and Youth with Autism Spectrum Disorders." *Journal of Autism and Developmental Disorders* 42, no. 2 (2011): 266-277. https://doi.org/10.1007/s10803-011-1241-x.

Carmassi, Claudia, et al. "Systematic Review of Sleep Disturbances and Circadian Sleep Desynchronization in Autism Spectrum Disorder: Toward an Integrative Model of a Self-Reinforcing Loop." *Frontiers in Psychiatry* 10, (2019). https://doi.org/10.3389/fpsyt.2019.00366.

Case-Smith, Jane, et al. "A Systematic Review of Sensory Processing Interventions for Children with Autism Spectrum Disorders." *Autism* 19, no. 2 (2014): 133-148. https://doi.org/10.1177/1362361313517762.

Chapman, Louise, et al. "'I Want to Fit In . . . but I Don't Want to Change Myself Fundamentally': A Qualitative Exploration of the Relationship between Masking and Mental Health for Autistic Teenagers." *Research in Autism Spectrum Disorders* 99, (2022). https://doi.org/10.1016/j.rasd.2022.102069.

Chapple, Melissa, et al. "Overcoming the Double Empathy Problem within Pairs of Autistic and Non-Autistic Adults through the Contemplation of Serious Literature." *Frontiers in Psychology* 12, (2021). https://doi.org/10.3389/fpsyg.2021.708375.

Charlton, Rebecca, et al. "'It Feels Like Holding Back Something You Need to Say': Autistic and Non-Autistic Adults Accounts of Sensory Experiences and Stimming." *Research in Autism Spectrum Disorders* 89, (2021). https://doi.org/10.1016/j.rasd.2021.101864.

Cheang, Rachel, et al. "Do You Feel Me? Autism, Empathic Accuracy and the Double Empathy Problem." *Autism*. (2024). https://doi.org/10.1177/13623613241252320.

Clément, Marc Andre, et al. "The Need for Sensory-Friendly 'Zones': Learning from Youth on the Autism Spectrum, Their Families, and Autistic Mentors Using a Participatory Approach." *Frontiers in Psychology* 13, (2022). https://doi.org/10.3389/fpsyg.2022.883331.

Cohen, Shana, et al. "'My Autism Is My Own': Autistic Identity and Intersectionality in the School Context." *Autism in Adulthood* 4, no. 4 (2022): 315-327. https://doi.org/10.1089/aut.2021.0087.

Conn, Carmel. "'Sensory Highs,' 'Vivid Rememberings,' and 'Interactive Stimming': Children's Play Cultures and Experiences of Friendship in Autistic Autobiographies." *Disability & Society* 30, no. 8 (2015): 1192-1206. https://doi.org/10.1080/09687599.2015.1081094.

Cook, Julia, et al. "Camouflaging in Autism: A Systematic Review." Center for Open Science. OSFPreprints (2021). https://doi.org/10.31219/osf.io/u5b9e.

Cook, Julia, et al. "Dropping the Mask: It Takes Two." *Autism* 28, no. 4 (2023): 831-842. https://doi.org/10.1177/13623613231183059.

Cooper, Kate, et al. "Social Identity, Self-Esteem, and Mental Health in Autism." *European Journal of Social Psychology* 47, no. 7 (2017): 844-854. https://doi.org/10.1002/ejsp.2297.

Corbett, Blythe, et al. "Comparing Cortisol, Stress, and Sensory Sensitivity in Children with Autism." *Autism Research* 2, no. 1 (2009): 39-49. https://doi.org/10.1002/aur.64.

Craddock, Emma. "Raising the Voices of AuDHD Women and Girls: Exploring the Co-Occurring Conditions of Autism and ADHD." *Disability & Society* 39, no. 8 (2024): 1-5. https://doi.org/10.1080/09687599.2023.2299342.

Crane, Laura, et al. "Parents' Views and Experiences of Talking about Autism with Their Children." *Autism* 23, no. 8 (2019): 1969-1981. https://doi.org/10.1177/1362361319836257.

Cresswell, Lily, et al. "The Experiences of Peer Relationships amongst Autistic Adolescents: A Systematic Review of the Qualitative Evidence. *Research in Autism Spectrum Disorders* 61, (2019): 45-60. https://doi.org/10.1016/j.rasd.2019.01.003.

Davidson, Joyce and Victoria Henderson. "'Coming Out' on the Spectrum: Autism, Identity, and Disclosure." *Social & Cultural Geography* 11, no. 2 (2010): 155-170. https://doi.org/10.1080/14649360903525240.

Davis, Mariya, et al. "A Systematic Review of Firsthand Experiences and Supports for Students with Autism Spectrum Disorder in Higher Education." *Research in Autism Spectrum Disorders* 84, (2021). https://doi.org/10.1016/j.rasd.2021.101769.

Dell'Osso, Liliana, et al. "Biological Correlates of Altered Circadian Rhythms, Autonomic Functions and Sleep Problems in Autism Spectrum Disorder." *Annals of General Psychiatry* 21, no. 1 (2022). https://doi.org/10.1186/s12991-022-00390-6.

Doherty, Mary, et al. "Autistic SPACE: A Novel Framework for Meeting the Needs of Autistic People in Healthcare Settings." *British Journal of Hospital Medicine* 84, no. 4 (2023): 1-9. https://doi.org/10.12968/hmed.2023.0006.

Duffus, Rebecca and Lyric Rivera. "What Autism Is My Autistic Identity: Interests and Focus." In *Autism, Identity and Me: A Professional and Parent Guide to Support a Positive Understanding of Autistic Identity.* Routledge, 2022.

Dwyer, Patrick, et al. "First Do No Harm: Suggestions Regarding Respectful Autism Language." *Pediatrics 149, no.* 4 (2022). https://doi.org/10.1542/peds.2020-049437n.

Dynia, Jaclyn, et al. "Addressing Sensory Needs for Children with Autism Spectrum Disorder in the Classroom." *Intervention in School and Clinic* 58, no. 4 (2023): 257-263. https://doi.org/10.1177/10534512221093786.

Elmose, Mette. "Understanding Loneliness and Social Relationships in Autism: The Reflections of Autistic Adults." *Nordic Psychology* 72, no. 1 (2019): 3-22. https://doi.org/10.1080/19012276.2019.1625068.

Esposito, Dario, et al. "Sleeping without Prescription: Management of Sleep Disorders in Children with Autism with Non-Pharmacological Interventions and Over-the-Counter Treatments." *Brain Sciences* 10, no. 7 (2020): 441. https://doi.org/10.3390/brainsci10070441.

Bibliography

Evans, Joshua, et al. "What You Are Hiding Could Be Hurting You: Autistic Masking in Relation to Mental Health, Interpersonal Trauma, Authenticity, and Self-Esteem." *Autism in Adulthood* 6, no. 2 (2024). https://doi.org/10.1089/aut.2022.0115.

Feng, Shuyuan, et al. "The Uncanny Valley Effect in Typically Developing Children and Its Absence in Children with Autism Spectrum Disorders." *Plos One* 13, no. 11 (2018). https://doi.org/10.1371/journal.pone.0206343.

Fiene, Lisa and Charlotte Brownlow. "Investigating Interoception and Body Awareness in Adults with and without Autism Spectrum Disorder." *Autism Research* 8, no. 6 (2015): 709-716. https://doi.org/10.1002/aur.1486.

Fletcher-Watson, Sue and Geoffrey Bird. "Autism and Empathy: What Are the Real Links?" *Autism* 24, no. 1 (2019): 3-6. https://doi.org/10.1177/1362361319883506.

Frost, Kyle et al. "'I Just Want Them to See Me As . . . Me'": Identity, Community, and Disclosure Practices among College Students on the Autism Spectrum." *Autism in Adulthood* 1, no. 4 (2019): 268-275. https://doi.org/10.1089/aut.2018.0057.

Gagnon, Katia, et al. "REM Sleep EEG Activity and Clinical Correlates in Adults with Autism." *Frontiers in Psychiatry* 12, (2021). https://doi.org/10.3389/fpsyt.2021.659006.

Ghaziuddin, Mohammad. "Suicide Rates in Adults with Autism." In *Encyclopedia of Autism Spectrum Disorders*, edited by Fred R. Volkmar. Springer, 2021. https://doi.org/10.1007/978-3-319-91280-6_455.

Gray, Sarah, et al. "Autistic Narratives of Sensory Features, Sexuality, and Relationships." *Autism in Adulthood* 3, no. 3 (2021): 238-246. https://doi.org/10.1089/aut.2020.0049.

Groenman, Annabeth, et al. "Menstruation and Menopause in Autistic Adults: Periods of Importance?" Center for Open Science. PsyArXiv Preprints. (2021). https://doi.org/10.31234/osf.io/kn8xe.

Grove, Rachel, et al. "Special Interests and Subjective Well-Being in Autistic Adults." *Autism Research* 11, no. 5 (2018): 766-775. https://doi.org/10.1002/aur.1931.

Grove, Rachel, et al. "The Motivation for Special Interests in Individuals with Autism and Controls: Development and Validation of the Special Interest Motivation Scale." *Autism Research* 9, no. 6 (2015): 677-688. https://doi.org/10.1002/aur.1560.

Hayward, Susan, et al. "Autism and Employment: What Works." *Research in Autism Spectrum Disorders* 60, (2019): 48-58. https://doi.org/10.1016/j.rasd.2019.01.006.

Hobson, R. Peter. "Autism, Literal Language and Concrete Thinking: Some Developmental Considerations." *Metaphor and Symbol* 27, no. 1 (2012): 4-21. https://doi.org/10.1080/10926488.2012.638814.

Horder, Jamie, et al. "Autistic Traits and Abnormal Sensory Experiences in Adults." *Journal of Autism and Developmental Disorders* 44, no. 6 (2013): 1461-1469. https://doi.org/10.1007/s10803-013-2012-7.

Howe, Fiona and Steven Stagg. "How Sensory Experiences Affect Adolescents with an Autistic Spectrum Condition within the Classroom." *Journal of Autism and Developmental Disorders* 46, no. 5 (2016): 1656-1668. https://doi.org/10.1007/s10803-015-2693-1.

Huang, Yunhe, et al. "Autistic Adults' Experiences of Diagnosis Disclosure." *Journal of Autism and Developmental Disorders* 52, (2022): 5301-5307. https://doi.org/10.1007/s10803-021-05384-z.

Jamero, Josephine. "Social Constructivism and Play of Children with Autism for Inclusive Early Childhood." *International Journal of Early Childhood Special Education* 11, (2019): 154-167. https://doi.org/10.20489/intjecse.670475.

Jobe, Lisa and Susan Williams White. "Loneliness, Social Relationships, and a Broader Autism Phenotype in College Students." *Personality and Individual Differences* 42, no. 8 (2007): 1479-1489. https://doi.org/10.1016/j.paid.2006.10.021.

Jones, Elizabeth, et al. "Distraction, Distress and Diversity: Exploring the Impact of Sensory Processing Differences on Learning and School Life for Pupils with Autism Spectrum Disorders." *Research in Autism Spectrum Disorders* 72, (2020). https://doi.org/10.1016/j.rasd.2020.101515.

Jury, Mickaël, et al. "Teachers' Attitudes toward the Inclusion of Students with Autism Spectrum Disorder: Impact of Students' Difficulties." *Research in Autism Spectrum Disorders* 83, (2021). https://doi.org/10.1016/j.rasd.2021.101746.

Kapp, Steven, et al. "'People Should Be Allowed to Do What They Like': Autistic Adults' Views and Experiences of Stimming." *Autism* 23, no. 7 (2019): 1782-1792. https://doi.org/10.1177/1362361319829628.

Kassee, Caroline, et al. "Physical Health of Autistic Girls and Women: A Scoping Review." *Molecular Autism* 11, no. 1 (2020). https://doi.org/10.1186/s13229-020-00380-z.

Kaydırak, Meltem, et al. "Effectiveness of Menstruation Hygiene Skills Training for Adolescents with Autism." *World Journal of Psychiatry* 13, no. 11 (2023): 958-966. https://doi.org/10.5498/wjp.v13.i11.958.

Kazek, Beata, et al. "Eating Behaviors of Children with Autism—Pilot Study, Part II." *Nutrients* 13, no. 11 (2021): 3850. https://doi.org/10.3390/nu13113850.

Khasnis, Namratha, et al. "Care-in-a-Cup: A Solution to Tend to the Needs of Autistic and Differently Abled Women." *2022 IEEE International Conference for Women in Innovation, Technology & Entrepreneurship.* https://doi.org/10.1109/icwite57052.2022.10176224.

Kilincaslan, Ayse, et al. "Daily Living Skills in Children with Autism Spectrum Disorder and Intellectual Disability: A Comparative Study from Turkey." *Research in Developmental Disabilities* 85, (2019): 187-196. https://doi.org/10.1016/j.ridd.2018.12.005.

Kinnaird, Emma, et al. "Investigating Alexithymia in Autism: A Systematic Review and Meta-Analysis." *European Psychiatry* 55, (2019): 80-89. https://doi.org/10.1016/j.eurpsy.2018.09.004.

Kirby, Anne, et al. "Sensory Experiences of Children with Autism Spectrum Disorder: In Their Own Words." *Autism* 19, no. 3 (2014): 316-326. https://doi.org/10.1177/1362361314520756.

Lachance, Kathryn. "Managing the Meltdown: Supporting Autistic Youth through Episodes." *The Brown University Child and Adolescent Behavior Letter* 40, no. 2 (2024): 1-4. https://doi.org/10.1002/cbl.30763.

Lai, Meng-Chuan, et al. "Prevalence of Co-Occurring Mental Health Diagnoses in the Autism Population: A Systematic Review and Meta-Analysis." *SSRN Electronic Journal.* (2019). https://doi.org/10.2139/ssrn.3310628.

Lake, Johanna, et al. "Mental Health Services for Individuals with High Functioning Autism Spectrum Disorder." *Autism Research and Treatment.* (2014): 1-9. https://doi.org/10.1155/2014/502420.

Lange, Stella. "Different Not Less: Neurodiversity As a Lens for Understanding Our Students Better." *Scope: Contemporary Research Topics.* Otago Polytechnic Press, 2022. https://doi.org/10.34074/scop.4011005.

Lewis, Laura and Kailey Stevens. "The Lived Experience of Meltdowns for Autistic Adults." *Autism* 27, no. 6 (2023): 1817-1825. https://doi.org/10.1177/13623613221145783.

Long, Rebecca. "Access Points: Understanding Special Interests through Autistic Narratives." *Autism in Adulthood* 7, no. 1 (2024). https://doi.org/10.1089/aut.2023.0157.

Lott-Sandkamp, Lea, et al. "Impairment in Reading Negative Social Cues Extends Beyond the Face in Autism." *Journal of Psychiatric Research* 164, (2023): 350-356. https://doi.org/10.1016/j.jpsychires.2023.06.032.

MacLennan, Keren, et al. "'It Is a Big Spider Web of Things': Sensory Experiences of Autistic Adults in Public Spaces." *Autism in Adulthood* 5, no. 4 (2023): 411-422. https://doi.org/10.1089/aut.2022.0024.

MacLennan, Keren, et al. "In Our Own Words: The Complex Sensory Experiences of Autistic Adults." *Journal of Autism and Developmental Disorders* 52, no. 7 (2021): 3061-3075. https://doi.org/10.1007/s10803-021-05186-3.

Mallory, Courtney and Brandon Keehn. "Implications of Sensory Processing and Attentional Differences Associated with Autism in Academic Settings: An Integrative Review." *Frontiers in Psychiatry* 12, (2021). https://doi.org/10.3389/fpsyt.2021.695825.

Mandy, Will. "Six Ideas about How to Address the Autism Mental Health Crisis." *Autism* 26, no. 2 (2022): 289-292. https://doi.org/10.1177/13623613211067928.

Mansour, Yusra, et al. "Central Auditory and Vestibular Dysfunction Are Key Features of Autism Spectrum Disorder." *Frontiers in Integrative Neuroscience* 15, (2021). https://doi.org/10.3389/fnint.2021.743561.

Martin, Rebekah and Julia Wilkins. "Creating Visually Appropriate Classroom Environments for Students with Autism Spectrum Disorder." *Intervention in School and Clinic* 57, no. 3 (2021): 176-181. https://doi.org/10.1177/10534512211014882.

Martin, Tara, et al. "Transitioning Primary School Students with Autism Spectrum Disorder from a Special Education Setting to a Mainstream Classroom: Successes and Difficulties." *International*

Journal of Inclusive Education 25, no. 5 (2019): 640-655. https://doi.org/10.1080/13603116.2019.1568597.

Matthew J. Maenner, et al. "Prevalence and Characteristics of Autism Spectrum Disorder among Children Aged Eight Years—Autism and Developmental Disabilities Monitoring Network, Eleven Sites, United States, 2020." *Surveillance Summaries* 72, no. 2 (2023): 1–14. https://doi.org/10.15585/mmwr.ss7202a1.

Mayes, Susan Dickerson, et al. "Suicide Ideation and Attempts in Children with Autism." *Research in Autism Spectrum Disorders* 7, no. 1 (2013): 109-119. https://doi.org/10.1016/j.rasd.2012.07.009.

Mazza, Monica, et al. "Affective and Cognitive Empathy in Adolescents with Autism Spectrum Disorder." *Frontiers in Human Neuroscience* 8, (2014). https://doi.org/10.3389/fnhum.2014.00791.

McDonald, T.A.M. "Autism Identity and the 'Lost Generation': Structural Validation of the Autism Spectrum Identity Scale and Comparison of Diagnosed and Self-Diagnosed Adults on the Autism Spectrum." *Autism in Adulthood* 2, no. 1 (2020): 13-23. https://doi.org/10.1089/aut.2019.0069.

McQuaid, Goldie, et al. "Camouflaging in Autism Spectrum Disorder: Examining the Roles of Sex, Gender Identity and Diagnostic Timing." Center for Open Science. PsyArXiv Preprints, (2021). https://doi.org/10.31234/osf.io/frbj3.

Milton, Damian, et al. "Autism and the 'Double Empathy Problem.'" In *Conversations on Empathy: Interdisciplinary Perspectives on Imagination and Radical Othering, edited by* Francesca Mezzenzana and Daniela Peluso. Taylor & Francis, 2023.

Mitchell, Peter, et al. "Autism and the Double Empathy Problem: Implications for Development and Mental Health." *British Journal of Developmental Psychology* 39, no. 1 (2021): 1-18. https://doi.org/10.1111/bjdp.12350.

Montaque, Indiana, et al. "'It Feels Like Something Difficult Is Coming Back to Haunt Me': An Exploration of 'Meltdowns' Associated with Autistic Spectrum Disorder from a Parental Perspective." *Clinical Child Psychology and Psychiatry* 23, no. 1 (2017): 125-139. https://doi.org/10.1177/1359104517730114.

Moore, Isobel, et al. The Intersection of Autism and Gender in the Negotiation of Identity: A Systematic Review and Metasynthesis." *Feminism & Psychology* 32, no. 4 (2022): 421-442. https://doi.org/10.1177/09593535221074806.

Mori, Masahiro, et al. "The Uncanny Valley [From the Field]." *IEEE Robotics & Automation Magazine* 19, no. 2 (2012): 98-100. https://www.researchgate.net/publication/254060168_The_Uncanny_Valley_From_the_Field.

Moseley, Rachel, et al. "Autism Research Is 'All about the Blokes and the Kids': Autistic Women Breaking the Silence on Menopause." *British Journal of Health Psychology* 26, no. 3 (2020): 709-726. https://doi.org/10.1111/bjhp.12477.

Nason, Bill. *The Autism Discussion Page on Stress, Anxiety, Shutdowns and Meltdowns: Proactive Strategies for Minimizing Sensory, Social and Emotional Overload.* Jessica Kingsley Publishers, 2019.

New Zealand Ministry of Social Development. *"Reasonable Accommodation."* Accessed April 5, 2025. https://www.msd.govt.nz/about-msd-and-our-work/work-programmes/lead-programme-work/information-and-support/reasonable-accommodation.html#:~:text=Employers%20must%20not%20discriminate%20against,services%20or%20facilities%20if%20needed.

Norris, Jade Eloise, et al. "Disclosing an Autism Diagnosis Improves Ratings of Candidate Performance in Employment Interviews." *Autism* 28, no. 4 (2023): 1045-1050. https://doi.org/10.1177/13623613231203739.

Nowell, Kerri, et al. "Characterization of Special Interests in Autism Spectrum Disorder: A Brief Review and Pilot Study Using the Special Interests Survey." *Journal of Autism and Developmental Disorders* 51, no. 8 (2020): 2711-2724. https://doi.org/10.1007/s10803-020-04743-6.

Nuske, Heather Joy, et al. "Broken Bridges—New School Transitions for Students with Autism Spectrum Disorder: A Systematic Review on Difficulties and Strategies for Success." *Autism* 23, no. 2 (2018): 306-325. https://doi.org/10.1177/1362361318754529.

Orsmond, Gael, et al. "Mother–Child Relationship Quality among Adolescents and Adults with Autism." *American Journal on Mental Retardation* 111, no. 2 (2006): 121. https://doi.org/10.1352/0895-8017(2006)111[121:mrqaaa]2.0.co;2.

Orsmond, Gael, et al. "Peer Relationships and Social and Recreational Activities among Adolescents and Adults with Autism." *Journal of Autism and Developmental Disorders* 34, no. 3 (2004): 245-256. https://doi.org/10.1023/b:jadd.0000029547.96610.df.

Papadopoulos, Nicole, et al. "Sleeping Sound with Autism Spectrum Disorder (ASD): Study Protocol for an Efficacy Randomised Controlled Trial of a Tailored Brief Behavioural Sleep Intervention for ASD." *BMJ Open* 9, no. 11 (2019). https://doi.org/10.1136/bmjopen-2019-029767.

Parmar, Ketan, et al. "Visual Sensory Experiences from the Viewpoint of Autistic Adults. *Frontiers in Psychology* 12, (2021). https://doi.org/10.3389/fpsyg.2021.633037.

Pearson, Amy and Kieran Rose. "A Conceptual Analysis of Autistic Masking: Understanding the Narrative of Stigma and the Illusion of Choice." *Autism in Adulthood* 3, no. 1 (2021): 52-60. https://doi.org/10.1089/aut.2020.0043.

Perry, Ella, et al. "Understanding Camouflaging As a Response to Autism-Related Stigma: A Social Identity Theory Approach." *Journal of Autism and Developmental Disorders* 52, no. 2 (2021): 800-810. https://doi.org/10.1007/s10803-021-04987-w.

Petrolini, Valentina, et al. "What Does It Take to be Rigid? Reflections on the Notion of Rigidity in Autism." *Frontiers in Psychiatry* 14, (2023). https://doi.org/10.3389/fpsyt.2023.1072362.

Phung, Jasmine, et al. "What I Wish You Knew: Insights on Burnout, Inertia, Meltdown, and Shutdown from Autistic Youth." *Frontiers in Psychology* 12, 2021. https://doi.org/10.3389/fpsyg.2021.741421.

Radulski, Elizabeth. "Conceptualising Autistic Masking, Camouflaging, and Neurotypical Privilege: Towards a Minority Group Model of Neurodiversity." *Human Development* 66, no. 2 (2022): 113-127. https://doi.org/10.1159/000524122.

Rapaport, Hannah, et al. "'I Live in Extremes': A Qualitative Investigation of Autistic Adults' Experiences of Inertial Rest and Motion." *Autism* 28, no. 5 (2023): 1305-1315. https://doi.org/10.1177/13623613231198916.

Ratner, Kaylin and Steven Berman. "The Influence of Autistic Features on Identity Development in Emerging Adults." *Emerging Adulthood* 3, no. 2 (2014): 136-139. https://doi.org/10.1177/2167696814559305.

Riccio, Ariana, et al. "How Is Autistic Identity in Adolescence Influenced by Parental Disclosure Decisions and Perceptions of Autism?" *Autism* 25, no. 2 (2020): 374-388. https://doi.org/10.1177/1362361320958214.

Riquelme, Immaculada, et al. "Abnormal Pressure Pain, Touch Sensitivity, Proprioception, and Manual Dexterity in Children with Autism Spectrum Disorders." *Neural Plasticity.* (2016): 1-9. https://doi.org/10.1155/2016/1723401.

Romualdez, Anna Melissa, et al. "'People Might Understand Me Better': Diagnostic Disclosure Experiences of Autistic Individuals in the Workplace." *Autism in Adulthood* 3, no. 2 (2021): 157-167. https://doi.org/10.1089/aut.2020.0063.

Romualdez, Anna Melissa, et al. "Autistic Adults' Experiences of Diagnostic Disclosure in the Workplace: Decision-Making and Factors Associated with Outcomes." *Autism & Developmental Language Impairments* 6, (2021). https://doi.org/10.1177/23969415211022955.

Sasson, Noah and Kerrianne Morrison. "First Impressions of Adults with Autism Improve with Diagnostic Disclosure and Increased Autism Knowledge of Peers." *Autism* 23, no. 1 (2017): 50-59. https://doi.org/10.1177/1362361317729526.

Schauder, Kimberly, et al. "Interoceptive Ability and Body Awareness in Autism Spectrum Disorder." *Journal of Experimental Child Psychology* 131, (2015): 193-200. https://doi.org/10.1016/j.jecp.2014.11.002

Schneid, Iris and Aviad Raz. "The Mask of Autism: Social Camouflaging and Impression Management As Coping/Normalization from the Perspectives of Autistic Adults." *Social Science & Medicine* 248, (2020). https://doi.org/10.1016/j.socscimed.2020.112826.

Sedgewick, Felicity, et al. "Friends and Lovers: The Relationships of Autistic and Neurotypical Women." *Autism in Adulthood* 1, no. 2 (2019): 112-123. https://doi.org/10.1089/aut.2018.0028.

Şengüzel, Seda, et al. "Impact of Eating Habits and Nutritional Status on Children with Autism Spectrum Disorder." *Journal of Taibah University Medical Sciences* 16, no. 3 (2021): 413-421. https://doi.org/10.1016/j.jtumed.2020.11.010.

Shah, Amita. *Catatonia, Shutdown and Breakdown in Autism: A Psycho-Ecological Approach.* Jessica Kingsley Publishers, 2019.

Shakes, Pieta and Andrew Cashin. "An Analysis of Twitter Discourse Regarding Identifying Language for People on the Autism Spectrum." *Issues in Mental Health Nursing 41*, no. 3 (2019): 221-228. https://doi.org/10.1080/01612840.2019.1648617.

Sibeoni, Jordan, et al. "The Sensory Experiences of Autistic people: A Metasynthesis." *Autism* 26, no. 5 (2022): 1032-1045. https://doi.org/10.1177/13623613221081188.

Singh, Asmita and Seo, Han-Seok. "Atypical Sensory Functions and Eating Behaviors among Adults on the Autism Spectrum: One-on-One Interviews." *Journal of Sensory Studies* 37, no. 2 (2021). https://doi.org/10.1111/joss.12724.

Sönmez, Dilruba and Timothy Jordan. "Investigating Associations between Cognitive Empathy, Affective Empathy and Anxiety in Adolescents with Autism Spectrum Disorder." *International Journal of Developmental Disabilities* 70, no. 5 (2023): 1-9. https://doi.org/10.1080/20473869.2022.2163605.

Spratt, Eve, et al. "Enhanced Cortisol Response to Stress in Children in Autism." *Journal of Autism and Developmental Disorders* 42, no. 1 (2011): 75-81. https://doi.org/10.1007/s10803-011-1214-0.

Stanford University Center for Sleep in Autism Spectrum Disorder. "Sleep and Autism." Accessed April 5, 2025. https://med.stanford.edu/csasd/education/parent-toolkit/parent-autistic-sleep.html.

Stark, Eloise, et al. "Autistic Cognition: Charting Routes to Anxiety." *Trends in Cognitive Sciences* 25, no. 7 (2021): 571-581. https://doi.org/10.1016/j.tics.2021.03.014.

Stephenson, Hanna, et al. "'I Know It's Very Spectrum-Y': Autistic Women Reflect on Sensory Aspects of Food and Eating." *Autism in Adulthood.* (2024). https://doi.org/10.1089/aut.2023.0114.

Strömberg, Maria, et al. "Experiences of Sensory Overload and Communication Barriers by Autistic Adults in Health Care Settings." *Autism in Adulthood* 4, no. 1 (2022): 66-75. https://doi.org/10.1089/aut.2020.0074.

Taboas, Amanda, et al. "Preferences for Identity-First Versus Person-First Language in a US Sample of Autism Stakeholders." *Autism 27*, no. 2 (2022): 565-570. https://doi.org/10.1177/13623613221130845.

Talcer, Moyna Catherine, et al. "A Qualitative Exploration into the Sensory Experiences of Autistic Mothers." *Journal of Autism and Developmental Disorders* 53, no. 2 (2021): 834-849. https://doi.org/10.1007/s10803-021-05188-1.

Thompson-Hodgetts, Sandra, et al. "Helpful or Harmful? A Scoping Review of Perceptions and Outcomes of Autism Diagnostic Disclosure to Others." *Research in Autism Spectrum Disorders* 77, (2020). https://doi.org/10.1016/j.rasd.2020.101598.

Toy, Harun, et al. "Autistic Traits in Women with Primary Dysmenorrhea: A Case-Control Study." *Neuropsychiatric Disease and Treatment* 12, (2016): 2319-2325. https://doi.org/10.2147/ndt.s114439.

Trundle, Grace, et al. "Prevalence of Victimisation in Autistic Individuals: A Systematic Review and Meta-Analysis. *Trauma, Violence, & Abuse* 24, no. 4 (2022): 2282-2296. https://doi.org/10.1177/15248380221093689.

Unwin, Katy, et al. "A Sequential Mixed-Methods Approach to Exploring the Experiences of Practitioners Who Have Worked in Multi-Sensory Environments with Autistic Children." *Research in Developmental Disabilities* 118, (2021). https://doi.org/10.1016/j.ridd.2021.104061.

Unwin, Katy, et al. "The Use of Multi-Sensory Environments with Autistic Children: Exploring the Effect of Having Control of Sensory Changes." *Autism* 26, no. 6 (2021): 1379-1394. https://doi.org/10.1177/13623613211050176.

Vousden, Bethany, et al. "The Play Skills of Children with High-Functioning Autism Spectrum Disorder in Peer-to-Peer Interactions with Their Classmates: A Multiple Case Study

Design." *Australian Occupational Therapy Journal* 66, no. 2 (2018): 183-192. https://doi.org/10.1111/1440-1630.12530.

Ward, Jamie, et al. "Atypical Sensory Sensitivity As a Shared Feature between Synaesthesia and Autism." *Scientific Reports* 7, no. 1 (2017). https://doi.org/10.1038/srep41155.

White, Rhianna, et al. "Is Disclosing an Autism Spectrum Disorder in School Associated with Reduced Stigmatization?" *Autism* 24, no. 3 (2019): 744-754. https://doi.org/10.1177/1362361319887625.

Williams, Kathryn et al. "Use of Sensory Adaptive Environments with Autistic Children: A Scoping Review." *Research in Autism Spectrum Disorders* 114, (2024). https://doi.org/10.1016/j.rasd.2024.102362.

Yamane, Kiyoko, et al. "Support and Development of Autistic Children with Selective Eating Habits." *Brain and Development* 42, no. 2 (2020): 121-128. https://doi.org/10.1016/j.braindev.2019.09.005.

Zajic, Matthew Carl and Juliette Gudknecht. "Person- and Identity-First Language in Autism Research: A Systematic Analysis of Abstracts from Eleven Autism Journals." *Autism* 28, no. 10 (2024). https://doi.org/10.1177/13623613241241202.

Index

A

accommodations, 110, 116–118, 120–122, 124

alexithymia, 61, 79, 103

allistic individuals, 40, 85, 91, 93, 131

anger, 73, 129

anxiety, causes of, 29, 40, 47, 49, 52, 61, 76–78, 80, 91, 145

aromas, 39, 41, 62

attention to detail, 32, 48, 52, 100, 107

autistic inertia, 140, 169

autistic students, 110–111, 113, 115–116

autonomous sensory meridian response (ASMR), 146

autonomy, 11, 111, 126

B

balance and movement, 54

beige diet, 36–37, 143

black-and-white thinking, 95, 97–99

board of trustees, 31, 97, 106, 118, 133

body language, 21, 77, 89–90, 105

burnout, 16–17, 102, 120

C

camouflaging, 15, 20–23, 29, 85–86

chewelry, 59

circadian rhythms, 147

classrooms, 45–46, 48, 110–112, 114, 120

clothing labels, 43

cognitive-behavioral therapy (CBT), 79, 146

communication, 42, 80, 86–87, 89–91, 101, 105, 118, 128

communities of autistic people, 9, 15, 28, 34, 84, 101–102, 119

cortisol, 77

coworkers, 53, 62, 66, 70

D

dangerous behaviors, 55, 57

deep pressure input, 59

deep pressure techniques, 53, 58

depression, 53, 75–76, 78–79

diagnosis of autism, 15–16, 19–20, 123, 125, 127, 129–130, 133
early, 34, 123

diet and food, 36, 38–39, 44, 143–144
meal preparation, 38, 45, 138–139, 142–143

disclosure of autism, 14, 124, 130

discrimination, 122–125
doctors, 11, 125

E
empathy, 92–93
employers, 114, 116–118,
121–122
equilibrium, 56–57, 63
ergonomic workstations, 117
executive function limitations,
154
exhaustion, 17, 29, 73
expressing emotions, 103–105,
107
eye contact, 21–22

F
facial expressions, 21–22, 86–90,
105
fainting, 63, 66
fears of autistic people, 23, 30,
53, 76, 122, 124–125
fidget toys, 26–27, 35, 71
friendships, 42, 84–85, 91,
94–97, 99, 119

G
gaslighting, 96

H
habituation, 50
happiness, 82, 88, 94, 107, 138
home maintenance, 137, 153, 155
hugging, 42, 58–59, 70–71

human resources departments,
121
hunger, 60, 62–63, 66
hydration, 63–64
hyperacusis, 49
hyperfocus, 81, 139–140
hypersensitive and hyposensitive,
35–37, 39, 45, 58, 112

I
identity
and clothing, 25
and community, 28
identity-first language, 8, 11–13,
18
inclusion, 79, 109, 131–132, 158
infantilization, 125–126
insomnia, 137, 145–147
interoception, 35, 60–63, 65–66,
139

J
job interviews, 117, 121

L
laughter, 90, 158
learning styles, 117
loneliness, 73, 106–107

M
medical professionals, 125, 152
meltdowns, 40, 46, 50–51,
69–73, 99, 110
menstruation, 151–153

Index

mental health, 17, 30, 34, 65, 75–77, 79, 81–82

mental health professionals, 75, 81

mental tendrils, 141

Milton, Damian, 93

mimicking, 21, 23, 86

mindfulness, 78

miscommunication, 69, 90

movement breaks, 113

music therapy, 79

N

neurodiversity, 7, 12, 14–15, 86–87, 117, 131, 157–159

noise, 36, 49, 51–52, 112

noise-cancelling headphones, 35–36, 51, 53, 67, 112, 154

O

Obsessive Compulsive Disorder (OCD), 9

P

pain thresholds, 65

parallel play, 93

personal hygiene, 137, 148–152, 155

person-first language, 8, 11–13, 18

picture guides, 150–151

prejudice, 124–25, 159

procrastination, 140

proprioception, 35, 56–59, 62, 70

R

rainbow shopping, 143

rapid eye movement (REM), 147

rejection sensitive dysphoria (RSD), 76–77

relational conflicts, 96, 104

romantic relationships, 97, 104

routines, 32, 53, 64, 76, 80, 99–100, 140

S

safe spaces, 70, 109, 111

sarcasm, 90

schools, 87, 109–13, 116

screaming, 49, 69, 140

scripted conversations, 21

self-acceptance, 12, 14, 26, 78, 129–132

self-esteem, 30, 82, 87, 130

sensory difficulties, 38, 110, 112, 145, 147, 153

sensory experiences

smell, 39–40

taste, 35–36, 38, 44

textures, 41, 43–44, 149

sensory overload, 37, 40–41, 46–48, 50–51, 75, 84, 113

shutdowns, 50–51, 69, 71–72

siblings of autistic people, 119

sign language, 9

sleep, 63–64, 66, 137–38, 140, 145–148, 155

medications, 146

YOU, ME, AND AUTISM

social situations, 22, 25, 30, 62, 77, 87, 97, 102
societal norms, 12, 23, 28, 83
SPACE model, 80
spatial awareness, 54, 56–57
special interests, 24–25, 81, 94
spoons method, 101–102
stigma, 14–15, 17–18, 71, 75, 78, 122–124, 127
stimming, 21, 26, 29, 40, 46, 51, 53
supermarket shopping, 154
support groups, 97, 118, 120, 129–130

T
tapping, 26, 54
teachers, 110–11, 113–114, 116
Temple Grandin, 87
tendril theory, 140, 150
therapists, 79–80, 103
time management, 115
transitions, 76, 99, 140–141, 150

U
uncanny valley effect, 85

V
vestibular system, 55
visual aids, 76, 79, 115, 141, 151–152
visual clutter, 45–46, 49, 112

W
weight control, 29, 38, 41
weighted blankets, 41, 58–59, 67, 70–71, 73, 147
work environments, 112–13, 117–118, 122, 124, 132
work opportunities, 115–116